Reflections fr

Reflecti

Mother's Kitchen

A Journey of Healing and Hope

Karen Malena

He restores my soul

Reflections from my Mother's Kitchen:

A Daughter's Memoir and Journey Towards Healing

© 2013 Karen Malena

Second Edition 2014 by Lamb Books

Contact the author at her website: http://karenmalena.com On Facebook: https://www.facebook.com/pages/Karen-Malena-author-page/318764301539139

Her Blog http://karenmalena.blogspot.com/
Goodreads
https://www.goodreads.com/author/show/5260052.Karen_Malena
Twitter
https://twitter.com/KarenLMalena
Pinterest
http://www.pinterest.com/karenmalena

ISBN-13:
978-0615989112 (Lamb Books)

ISBN-10:
061598911X

Reflections from my Mother's Kitchen

DEDICATION

This book is dedicated to my mom,

Eileen, (aka Ellen in this book)

and the countless hours spent in her kitchen with

incredible baked goods and deep, heartfelt conversation.

I love you, Mom.

Reflections from my Mother's Kitchen

TABLE OF CONTENTS

	Acknowledgments	i
	Prologue	1
1	Pietro's Song	3
2	Terry's Gift	35
3	Christmas Angel	69
4	Matthew's Courage	107
5	Potter's Clay	141
6	Ever After	189
	Recipes	
	Wine Cookies	217
	Lemon Knots	218
	Italian Easter Bread	219
	About the Author	221

ACKNOWLEDGMENTS

First and foremost, I'd like to start by thanking God for an incredible journey.

The black and white photo on the cover is the real Pietro, my great-grandfather. It is this beautiful picture that inspired me to seek family history and begin this journey of love, of sharing my family with you all.

A special thank you to my parents and brother for their love and support through the years, and having such awesome stories in our own lives to "fictionalize" in a book.

I'd like to thank my writer's group, Pittsburgh East Scribes for their tireless efforts, great edits and critique, and especially author Karen Anna Vogel for encouragement and help. Also author Michele Poydence for awesome suggestions.

A very special thank you to my husband, Jim, who as always, is my first listener and reviewer.

Please visit my blogs at karenmalena.blogspot.com for more inspirational stories from the heart.

Email me at scoutfinch15003@yahoo.com

Prologue

$\mathcal{A}$ blank sheet lay open before me. A slight breeze riffled the pages of the journal I clutched in my hands. The white wicker swing in dire need of a new paint job rocked lazily back and forth in time to the rhythm of my feet, and the sun hid behind a cloud making me shiver a little, but not from a chill. Mistakes from my past, self-doubt and insecurity nestled into my brain. They pulled up a chair and made themselves at home.

You failed at a marriage, they said. *You weren't good enough for him. You should have known better.*

You wasted time on a safe career instead of taking some risks and seeing what could have been, what should have been.

You're afraid of us, yet you embrace us. You'll never change.

I had fought the voices many times: I'm not who you say I am. I'm so much more.

Oh? You're practically middle-aged now. Do you really think you can change?

I tapped my pen against the paper. I hadn't been able to write one word today. Though years separated me from the times in my life I wanted to forget, could I return to the moments that shaped who I am now? In visiting the past, would I come to know more about myself than I ever dreamed possible?

I longed for the most familiar of places, the warmth of my mother's kitchen. It was there I hoped to finally find the answers and move on into the life I always dreamed I could live and become the person I always was meant to be.

.

Chapter 1

~~~

Pietro's Song

August, 2000

A simple black and white photograph and my life would never be the same.

I looked into eyes, haunting eyes which stared back at me from the old, worn snapshot, a slight smile turning up the corners of the sensual mouth. High cheekbones set into a handsome face, and a deep cleft in the strong chin.

His hands, workers hands, beautiful, and long fingered. The old, stained coveralls resplendent with wood dust, a carpenter's trademark.

What was on his mind when the photograph was taken? Thoughts of his wife and children? Thoughts of prosperity and good fortune in the new world?

What year did he arrive in this country? His whole life before him.

How long did the boat trip take, the nauseating, unending trip? A ship crammed full of other immigrants like him. Did he know some of the other passengers as he travelled? People packed tightly together like too many sardines in their metal prison of a can.

Who was he, really? What legacy did he leave?

The questions plagued me one summer day while I sat in the comfort of my mother's kitchen sifting through dozens of black and white photos. Some faded so badly, I could barely make out the ghostly figures. The cardboard box they were stored in sat off to the side a little worse for wear. Strips of peeled masking tape hung from the bulging edges, so yellowed from age I wondered how long Mom had kept these treasures.

"Why didn't you show me these before?" I asked, delicately sipping at the steaming mug of coffee Mom had set before me on the table. I was forty years old, and although Mom and I shared so many things and I knew some stories from her own youth, I had never met the rest of the "family," these old, Italian people who never seemed to smile in photographs.

"I was cleaning out my bedroom closet," Mom said. She stood near the stove, an oven mitt in one hand while the kitchen timer ticked out its last minutes. She'd invited me over for cinnamon rolls this morning. Mom was in her seventies now and although her body and mind were slowing down, her culinary skills were not. At least once a week, she'd pull out the old tin box of recipes and get down to some serious baking. Bowls and wooden spoons lay atop her counter, gobs of batter clinging to them.

It was a Saturday, I was off work, and it was a lovely summer day. My recent job as editor at The Plum Daily Times kept me from visiting my parents more frequently. Dad was gone for the morning, spending time with his old friend Jimmy Castillo at Della's Café, a small greasy spoon establishment in my parents' town. When Dad got together with his cronies, we wouldn't see him for hours. This was precious one- on- one time with my mother today.

Our talks were becoming a soothing ritual. Many days, when I was younger, I sat in this very kitchen, telling Mom about a boyfriend who'd slighted me or some hateful thing a girl in school said. Time after time she would patiently comfort me, recanting her own stories from youth. We would laugh together and sometimes cry, but we would always learn something from one another.

"Yeah," Mom continued, "Every time I opened my closet, something would fall on my head. Too many piles of junk in there from over the years, especially your father's stuff. That man's killing me, Kate, with his arts and crafts. Anyway, that box of pictures was stuck way in the back."

The timer pinged, and I smiled to myself thinking of my parents' relationship; Mom's crankiness, Dad's soft-spoken ways and the years of love between them. Mom pulled fresh cinnamon rolls from the oven, laying them carefully upon the counter. The heavenly aroma tickled my nose, and I jumped up to grab one, burning my fingers on the glaze of sugar. I sucked my wounded digits and sat back down to continue studying family members I would never know.

This photograph in particular had caught my eye and piqued my interest. A handsome young man wearing overalls, standing before a wooden building of some sort, his face and hands dirty from hard work. His eyes. . . I asked Mom about him.

"That's my grandfather," Mom said. "I told you a little

about him before, Kate. I never knew him though, only stories from my mother and aunts."

My mother began to tell me about my great-grandfather, Pietro, who would not live to see his fiftieth birthday. "He was a good man," she said. "So kind and gentle. I hear he treated my grandmother like a queen."

She stood with her back against the counter, arms crossed in front of her, a faraway look in her eyes while she recounted the few facts she knew of him.

He died of pneumonia, an illness so easily curable by today's standards, but in the 1930's, a death sentence.

He was the second brother to arrive in America in the early 1900's from Patrica, Italy, a small town near the foothills of Rome. He left a wife and three small children behind, hoping to find work and send for them once he was settled. It couldn't have been easy venturing into a land he didn't know much about, leaving his beloved town, farm land and customs, even though poverty constantly beckoned at the door.

Mom recanted stories she'd heard of how her grandfather had been the one to shyly explain the facts of life to his children, knowing his wife would be unable to, with her timid, backward ways.

Wow, I thought to myself. That couldn't have been easy, especially back in the day. I shuddered to picture the type of discussion my own father and I might have had and how uncomfortable it would have been.

Mom also heard stories of how her grandfather made homemade pasta himself, teaching his daughters at an early age, since her grandmother had been such a poor cook.

The most unsettling story of all circulated about some thugs who came to his door one day to roughhouse my great-grandfather. Never one for trouble, he claimed it had to be a mistake, and they had wrongly accused him of some sort of gambling debt. He carefully explained to them he wasn't their man. The next day, as my great-grandfather left the house for work, a smeared, tarry imprint of a black hand defaced the wooden siding of his home. A note pinned against the doorframe said the men would hurt him and every member of his family if he was lying. Pietro had gone to the foreman in the steel mill he worked in that day, who'd allegedly been a leader of some type of organized crime. Tearfully he told the man what happened. The foreman liked my great-grandfather and told him he would take care of the situation.

"Here's one," Mom said, walking over to the table, picking up a faded photo. "See, this is my grandfather standing in front of the house he built with his bare hands." She leaned over me while I stared unbelievingly. The three story brick, stone and wood home was enormous.

"His bare hands?" I asked. "Come on, Mom, I mean really?"

"Yes, I'm serious," she said. "He was one of the best carpenters and brick layers in the area, I was told." Mom grabbed her own cinnamon roll, one which had cooled down. "A big, strong man too from the look of him," she said, taking a bite of the roll.

I stopped for a moment, slathering butter atop my own pastry, savoring the delectable sweetness in my mouth. I wiped my hands on a napkin Mom handed me, careful not to dirty the precious, old photos.

Again I'm drawn to the photo of my great-grandfather, where he's standing alone. Never one to care much for family history, I am now hungry for knowledge, and starved for all I can find out. This man intrigued me. He looked poor, but with an unshakable confidence. His clothing was tattered and old, but he carried himself with pride. Serenity seemed to emanate from his very appearance. A figure larger than life.

Was it his faith perhaps? Did he believe so strongly in God, knowing He would take care of him when he came to this country trying to find work and a better life for his wife and children? Was he guilty perhaps of the debt he'd been accused of? Had he gotten into some sort of trouble, leaving his family open to disgrace? So many questions.

I kissed Mom and Dad goodnight later that evening, clutching several of the old photographs tightly to myself. As I drove away in my car, I couldn't stop thinking about the man, my great-grandfather and wanted to find out all I could about him.

Two furry cats greeted me at the door when I arrived home that evening. After throwing a few salmon treats their way, I holed up in my study for the night. I flipped open my laptop, looking at the pictures spread across my desk. My husband and son were away for the week visiting my in- laws. There would be no distractions. I sat sipping Riesling, running my fingers around the rim of the glass for a moment.

"Pietro." I said the name aloud. It sounded wonderful

to me. *Peter, the rock, like in the Bible.* Yes, I thought, very appropriate.

I typed his name into the search engine on my computer. Ellis Island records popped up instantly. I couldn't believe my good fortune. With a few deft clicks, I found facts that perhaps no one in the family had ever known. I found his birth year: 1889. I found the name of the ship he arrived on: The *Albert Konig* which departed from Naples, Italy in March of 1909. There were at least nine hundred passengers aboard the ship. Their quarters were in steerage, the "poor" section. He was twenty years of age when he came to this country. And he settled in my hometown of Ambridge, Pennsylvania.

All of a sudden, I sat a little straighter. I felt proud of this man, this Christopher Columbus who marked the way for me and my family. *You didn't even know anyone, yet you came, hoping for a better life.*

The next day, I called cousins and aunts, anyone who might have a shred of information for me about Pietro. I spoke with people I hadn't talked with in years, and heard a few more tales, a few more stories about this good man. I became obsessed, and thought of little else during the day. I desperately wished I had known him.

When I went to sleep that night, I clutched his picture to my chest. I thanked him and I thanked God for being born into this family, a family who had such a strong patriarch to guide us.

A lump formed in my throat and I held back tears which threatened to spill out of my eyes. I could see him, young and strong. I could see him, almost. . .

~*~

Waves pounded the old ship, the sound deafening as he leaned over the bow, transfixed by deep blue water in the early morning light. The smell of the ocean salt stung the air, sprays of it hitting his face, the taste of it bitter in his mouth. His worn pocket knife, sliced into a juicy apple, the liquid dribbling down the strong chin. Pietro's stomach growled a bit from hunger. He had shared the last of his bread with someone, a skeletal man who appeared to need it more than he did.

He shivered in the early morning chill, throwing the apple core over the railing, and pulled his worn coat more tightly about him. It was March, and many of the passengers stayed below in their cramped quarters. Too cold, they said. Why bother? But Pietro liked the freedom of strolling in the fresh air.

Many of the deckhands were busy nearby. Some washing and scrubbing, others repairing and adjusting instruments, pouring over charts. In some ways, Pietro felt useless. He wished he could help them somehow. He wasn't used to all this free time, this endless waiting.

He spent most of his days walking on the deck of the bulking ship, whistling or playing the old harmonica he kept in a pocket of his overalls. He didn't speak much for he was a quiet man, inner strength his best quality. Robust and healthy at twenty years old, a full life ahead of him, Pietro thanked God above for the opportunity to travel to a new country, hoping to find good work.

It had been three weeks already. Three long weeks since he had seen his wife, Adelina. Too much time since he had held his beloved children on his knee.

Images flooded him, the last, a sweet kiss Adelina gave him while the three little ones clung to her long apron, crying. "Don't go, Papa." Waving goodbye to them while he walked down the rocky, cobblestone path, his heart breaking.

Ah, Adelina will do well, he thought to himself. *She is strong and skilled at gardening, baking, and mending, everything needed to run a small household. Her mama and papa live nearby.*

It is a short walk to our small home. They will help her if need be.

Pietro's heart ached while he thought of her beautiful arms, tanned brown from long days in the sun and her lovely face, careworn at times. *Ti voglio bene. I love you.*

~*~

Sleep did not come easily that night as Pietro lay in the cramped quarters, thinking. Would there be enough work for him? Would his brother have enough room for him? How long would it be before he could send word to his family to join him?

Gazing into the darkness, he pulled a thin, threadbare blanket up under his chin and sighed. It hadn't been easy, the endless days and nights of ship travel. Not knowing a soul, loneliness a constant companion.

Times were tough in his hometown of Patrica, Italy. Born into poverty, barely able to make ends meet, he had heard of his countrymen striking out to seek life in the new world. Pietro knew there had to be a better way. With endless days of hard labor in the fields, sometimes crops so sparse, his family went to bed many nights with hunger in their bellies. He was tired of being poor. He prayed to God every day to show him the way.

Pietro reached under the tiny, wooden bunk and pulled

out his burlap sack clutching it almost lovingly to himself. It was filled with apples, dried beans, tomato seeds, green and red pepper seeds and the most delectable fruit of all, his dried figs. He was a farmer and had tilled the land of his beloved town since he was a young boy. He'd miss the gnarled fig tree, the one he buried underneath the soil each winter to preserve until the next year.

There will be new planting in America. My new crops will be larger than anything I have ever dreamed of.

He knew another skill: carpentry. His own papa, a carpenter by trade, taught young Pietro skills of building homes, hand-made furniture and beautiful, carved statues.

He thought about his brother, Carmen, who already lived in the United States. Would he be able to find him? The letters which were scrawled in Carmen's poor handwriting arrived at least three times a year. But Pietro hadn't heard from his brother in over six months now. He patted the pocket where important papers were kept, the ones with the names of the town and street his brother lived on.

Ambridge, Pennsylvania, U.S.A. What made his brother choose such a place? He knew it was near enough to the coal mines, and new steel plants which sprouted up like weeds amidst the vast country. Plenty of work, his brother had said, backbreaking labor.

I'm young, and strong.

A baby wailed, the sound droning on in the middle of the night. Pietro turned over onto his side and said a prayer for the infant and mother. *Poor little one.* He heard the sound of a hushed lullaby, and then the sweet sound of suckling. Someone else coughed an endless, harsh barking cough. Pietro will ask tomorrow who it is. He will share his meager meal with the man. But for now, sleep finally overtakes him.

The next day brought the storm, a mighty wind, heavy, torrential rain, pounding thunder, and a myriad of lightning. Children huddled closer to their mamas in their cramped quarters while Pietro played his harmonica, a haunting, Italian melody which calmed the little ones. An earsplitting crash resounded overhead while the immigrants huddled together.

"Move, move, move," a voice barked. A young shipmate rushed into their small space, motioning for the people to move quickly. He pointed feverishly to a staircase near the back of the ship, speaking words they couldn't understand.

Pietro picked up two small children, one in each, muscular arm, while a tired, young woman smiled her gratitude. People rushed forward, fear etched into their faces as they scrambled upward.

Lightning had struck a portion of their ship. A small fire raged on deck. The ensigns hurried to snuff it out. Pietro gently set the children at their mama's feet, and rushed to be of assistance. Other strong men followed, averting the crisis.

Cheers went up throughout the ship, while the captain wiped his brow with a worn, linen handkerchief. He thanked the men who willingly helped. Later, he shared tender beef and boiled potatoes with some of them. Pietro's belly was full and rest came much easier that night.

Pietro patted the brass harmonica in his overall pocket, the most precious gift his father had ever given him. Music soothes, his papa had told him. Music is from God. It made him smile to think of his music calming the children as the storm raged and how his own *figli*, little ones, loved it so.

A new day. The sun shone brightly. People lined up for bowls of bread sopping in thin milk. Pietro took his portion to the emaciated man, the one who coughed so violently each night. With gratitude, the man looked up into Pietro's piercing, green eyes, and a smile broke out onto the creased face. Pietro patted the man's shoulder, and walked away, whistling a tune his own dear mama had taught him many years ago. *"Tu Scendi Dalle Stelle*, You Fall From The Stars." He felt good.

The rowdy sound of raised voices piqued Pietro's curiosity and he approached several men who sat around a worn, wooden table. He watched as they played the card game all Italian men knew, *"Scopa."* His papa had warned him of the dangers of games. Money was precious and tight. Gambling was not allowed in their family. Pietro chuckled a little to himself, watching them play for buttons and embroidery thimbles. Their wives would curse them later if they lost precious sewing items.

A bottle of dark red vino, half empty, passed between the men. The smell of fermented grapes lay heavily in the air, and stains of purple adorned their worn undershirts. Pietro walked on, his harmonica playing a jaunty tune.

~*~

It had been weeks since he saw land. The days were long and the air biting with cold in the March winds. The nights were freezing, as people huddled close together in the cramped quarters for warmth. Yet every day, Pietro awakened renewed that this might be the day land was spotted in the distance. He walked back and forth upon the upper deck of the ship. *It is close now. I can feel it, I can smell it. Something is in the air.*

He fingered the wooden rosary, worn from many days and nights of prayers. It comforted him as- whispering sweet prayers for his family. *Grazie, Dio. God, grant them security. Grant me the courage in the new land to make a better life for them.*

It was midday when the lookout cried out, "Land, ho!" Excitement filled the ship as the news passed from person to person.

Pietro turned quickly, a sight in the distance he thought he'd never see. Buildings, tall and wide, the statue he had heard about many times before. *She is beautiful, Lady Liberty.* The spires of her crown pointed majestically in the air, the torch clasped firmly in her lovely hand. Pietro, overcome by emotions, pulled his handkerchief from his pocket and wept for joy.

Women, children and men arrived on deck, crowding around the rail as the captain and his officers looked on.

Hats were tossed into the air. Arms waved wildly. Small children asked questions, while excited parents tried to answer as whoops and shouts of excitement broke out from end to end of the massive ship.

In his mind's eye, Pietro could almost see his brother and family waiting for him. He saw beloved Carmen, ten years older than he, with a fancy suit and fancy bow tie, dapper cap upon his head. Elegant silk handkerchief sticking from the breast pocket of his suit. His wife, Elsa, fat and happy with a brocade dress and shiny, new shoes. Their three little children holding on to new toys, clutching them for dear life.

A hand upon his shoulder broke his reverie. "I want to thank you, young man," the man said in Italian. "You gave up your food to me many days. I will remember you."

A man of few words, Pietro smiled shyly at him, shaking his head as if to say it was nothing. They stood together as the ship drew nearer to the precious land.

~*~

It took hours for the passengers to depart. Luggage pulled from compartments, names read for the multitude to claim their meager belongings. Pietro carried very little, only one small leather bag with two pairs of pants, a new shirt, and his beloved satchel of figs, seeds and apples. He held them to himself, as he neared the ramp which would bring him to his new life.

It is time. Pietro started the lonely journey down the wooden plank to the sandy shore below. Such colors! He thought to himself. For he had never seen women dressed in such finery in his life. Such smells! There were vendors barking of the delectable foods they prepared as the hungry crowd departed the ship. Pietro's stomach growled, his mouth watered. He fingered the few *soldi* coins he had in the pocket of his overalls. *I'm so hungry.*

He passed by the vendors. He needed his few, precious coins.

Pietro and the other passengers were ushered into a large, gray building, a medical facility and processing center. Doctors in their white coats and pretty nurses in white dresses and caps called out names.

Several serious-looking men sat behind massive desks, lines of people before them. The questions were read from a paper, a translator nearby, "What is your name? Why are you here? Do you have any family members waiting for you? Do you have a criminal record?" When his turn arrived, Pietro patiently answered, remaining calm.

Another line to stand in. He heard his name called, Pietro Chiccerelli. He held a slip of paper high in the air and a nurse walked over to him, her smile warm and friendly. She escorted him into a room filled with many of the others he recognized from the ship.

A bald, heavy-set doctor walked up to him and motioned for Pietro to unbutton his shirt. The doctor listened to Pietro's chest with a cold shiny metal device he'd never seen before. The doctor peered into his eyes, ears and mouth, then wrote notes on a clipboard he retrieved from a desk piled high with papers and documents. Satisfied, the doctor dismissed him as an Italian translator told Pietro he had a clean bill of health.

Pietro was sent to yet another group of people who stood near a counter, with several dour-looking men exchanging money. His few, precious *soldi*, coins, were turned into pennies and nickels, strange looking coins.

He gave papers to the translator and was shown the direction of the train station. He followed a group of people, whistling.

~*~

Pietro stood before the massive, black engine as smoke billowed out, and he jumped as the train's whistle blew several times. He handed his boarding pass to a young man, entering the train that would take him to his new home.

It would be two more days before he arrived in the town of Ambridge. He hoped Carmen remembered the dates he had given him. Pietro relaxed against the seat, while the rhythm of the train lulled him to sleep.

In his dreams he was planting a garden, one bigger than anything he'd ever seen. His rake sliced into the earth, the sack of seeds slung from his tired shoulders as he dropped the precious pods into the ground. Other people worked near him, each with their own satchels, each with sweat pouring down their brow, but gladness in their hearts. Pietro mopped his own face with a red bandana, and gazed at the vast garden before him. Adelina came out onto the back porch of the wooden house before him, little Angela, Louisa and Samuel skipping alongside their mama. Pietro broke into a run, his heart bursting with joy at seeing his family.

The dream ended as the train jolted to a stop. Pietro sat up, feeling the lingering happiness at seeing his love again. *Soon, Adelina, soon.* His mouth was dry, his tongue stuck to the roof of his mouth. *"Aqua?"* he asked the man sitting next to him. The man shook his head, an emphatic "no."

~*~

Downtown Pittsburgh, Pennsylvania, U.S.A. The train chugged away gushing smelly smoke from its stack, as Pietro and the others stood with their baggage at the platform of the station. So many people, everyone looking as if they had somewhere important to go.

"*Mi scusi,*" he said, pulling his precious slip of paper, the one with the name of the town he was looking for. A uniformed policeman grabbed the slip with white, gloved hands and motioned with his arm to a sign which read "Departures." The officer held up two fingers in Pietro's face, and did this twice. "Number twenty- two," he said.

Pietro stared blankly at the police officer. He didn't understand the words. He shrugged his shoulders in a gesture of surrender and the cop, with a look of pity, gently guided him down the platform.

They neared a dais, the number twenty- two clearly marked, when Pietro finally understood. He nodded to the policeman, thanking him again and again. "*Grazie, grazie.*"

~*~

The connecting train chugged along the track, past the

city through towns with names like Emsworth, Bellevue, and Sewickley. In some ways, the countryside resembled his hometown, rolling hills, heavily wooded areas. Pietro felt alert and focused as he headed to the new town he'd call home.

He had never been on trains before this day, and it felt so free to him this strange, new way to travel. The train slowed, its whistle blew as it came to a complete stop several hours later. Pietro and the others departed into a small train station.

Pietro looked around, the chill of the March air making him shiver. The first steel mill he'd ever seen, American Bridge Company occupied the land behind the train station. A vast structure, not quite completed, it still looked fully operational. Huge smoke stacks billowed out gray smoke; men ran from place to place, their wheelbarrows filled with scraps of metal, faces black with soot and dust.

A sign, "Welcome to Ambridge" perched atop a small hillside. Pietro began the long walk into a downtown area past markets, a theater, clothing stores and a bank.

At a crossroad, Pietro looked around. *Where do I go? What do I do?* A streetcar rushed by, its clanging bell

25

scaring him.

He pulled another slip of paper from his pocket and tried to find a helpful soul, someone who could read the words scrawled upon it. People passed him, not bothering to even look.

It had been at least a day since he had something to eat or drink, and he sat dejectedly upon a wooden bench, plucking an apple from his satchel. The crisp, tart flavor only made his stomach growl more.

A young man and woman walked by with a baby sleeping peacefully in her buggy. Pietro stood, thrusting the slip of paper at the man. *"Mi scusi,"* he said, and gestured to the address printed upon it.

The man spoke to his wife quickly in American, then motioned for Pietro to follow them. "Come on, fellow," the young man said in the strange, new language. "It's not very far. We'll show you the way." Pietro didn't understand a word, but the excited way the man gestured and pointed, Pietro realized he was headed in the right direction.

Pietro followed them, tired now from hours, days and weeks of travel. All he wanted was to have one night of uninterrupted sleep.

They walked on in a comfortable silence, the baby waking up and cooing. It made Pietro's heart ache; he missed his little Louisa, the youngest, so much. They walked past the new stores, owners barking of their wares and finery. They headed into a lightly populated area, dotted with small, wooden homes. Clotheslines draped across yards on this March afternoon, another sight which tugged at his heart.

Up a steep hill they climbed, a large, brick school building on their left, a church with a steeple to their right. Pietro took it all in, the sights, the sounds of his new town. On they climbed, higher and higher up the crest of the hill. The man stopped and pointed to a wooden pole with a sign attached at the top. He pointed to the paper, and realization dawned on Pietro. The words matched: Pine Street. This is where his brother lived.

"*Grazie,*" he said to the couple. A few tears trickled from his eyes as he wiped them away with the back of one hand. He motioned for them to wait and produced two shiny apples for each of them from his satchel. The couple shook their head no, but he insisted. The young woman hugged him briefly, and gave him a small kiss on his cheek.

He passed clapboard homes and tightly packed row houses with small numbers on their doors. He was looking for number 427. He was sweating despite the cold, his armpits sticky with perspiration. His aching arms felt as if he carried two lead weights.

Suddenly, Pietro saw it. A tiny, white painted wood house, sagging porch and small, weedy yard. Could this possibly be the home of his rich, American brother? Disappointment hit him like a huge slap as Carmen stepped out onto the porch, smoking his hand-rolled cigarette, wearing clothes that looked like the ones on Pietro's own back. *The land of opportunity.* Not exactly what he'd pictured.

Recognition dawned on Carmen's face; he threw the cigarette onto the sidewalk and approached his brother. "*Mama mia!*" he exclaimed, hugging his brother tightly to his chest. Both men cried tears of joy.

Elsa walked out onto the porch in a tattered dress, a dishrag in her chubby hands. She squealed with delight as Pietro and Carmen mounted the concrete steps to their home. She babbled in Italian, hugging Pietro. Three dirty children surrounded him, poking into his satchel.

The aromas emanating from the kitchen tantalized Pietro as he walked into the house. It had been weeks since he had a real meal. Almost faint with hunger, he laid his baggage down, and followed Elsa into the kitchen. Fresh baked bread, sausages, and pasta fagioli. The meal looked like a feast to Pietro. Elsa laid an extra place for him and motioned for Pietro to sit. She ladled the steaming bean soup into their bowls. Carmen sliced into the warm bread, a dish of olive oil for dipping in the center of the table.

Carmen gave a word of thanks for the safe arrival of his younger brother. The children giggled while they watched their uncle dig into his plate with relish.

~*~

Later, when dishes were cleared and washed, the children in bed, Pietro and Carmen went out to the porch together.

Carmen motioned for his brother to sit upon a wooden crate that served as the porch's only seat. Pietro took a seat and tried to play a pleasant tune on his harmonica. It shocked Pietro to see the poor conditions around him. His brother was fortunate to have one of the few small homes in the area, when so many others lived in the close quarters of the row houses. So far Americans weren't much different than the poor of Italy.

"I know it isn't much, brother," Carmen said in Italian, blowing smoke through his nostrils. "But I have heard about plentiful work, the steel factory, coal mines in nearby West Virginia, and there may even be work for someone like you with your skilled labor. New buildings spring up like weeds." Carmen gestured with his hands high in the air, the cigarette dangling from the corner of his mouth. "Trust me, my brother, we will do well here. Give it time."

Pietro looked into the night sky, stars shimmering in brilliance. He made a wish on a falling star. *I want to do so much more than my papa. I want to be the one to break the curse of poverty in my family.*

"I am so tired," Pietro said, rising to his feet with a huge jaw- cracking yawn. "Please brother, show me where I may sleep."

Carmen brought his brother to a small room near the kitchen, a tangle of blankets on the floor, his makeshift bed. After saying goodnight to one another, Pietro said his prayers, and then lay upon the blankets falling instantly to sleep.

~*~

The summer months flew by while Pietro worked long hours. His back ached, his arms and legs tight from lengthy days shoveling coal for the furnaces of the American Bridge Company, his first job. At night, he sat at the workbench in his makeshift carpentry shop, the shed behind his brother's house, mending furniture for people in the town.

Weekends, he and his brother labored, beginning construction on new homes. They could barely keep up with the work that flooded them and four hours of sleep a night weren't nearly enough. But the thought pressed ever on: *This is for you, Adelina.*

People in the town began to hear of this hard-working man, the one with the magic hands, the stocky, Italian man who was known to play his harmonica on the way to his jobs.

~*~

By the time spring rolled around the following year, Pietro sat and wrote the most important letter of his life. The letter to Adelina.

My dearest wife:

It is with a glad heart I write to you. I have done it, my darling.

I have made a name for myself in America. I have a small home for us and our children. I have a garden that makes the one back home appear small. I am ready for you now, my love. Ready for you and our children to join me. My heart is happy. I await your letter.

Your love, Pietro

~*~

In June of 1911, another ship, the *Verona*, docked at Ellis Island. A woman with a pretty, yet careworn face departed with three small children clinging to her long skirts. Their faces were filled with fear, yet also with the light of hope. When they arrived on the train in Ambridge, Pennsylvania, Pietro was there to greet them, running to them, kissing his precious children, his beautiful wife. . .

~*~

I sat back at my desk upon finishing the manuscript about my great- grandfather. I wanted to go on forever speculating about his early life. But it was here I ended his tale.

I drove back to Ambridge again, this time with a heavy heart. I had looked up cemetery records, you see, and found his grave. I never knew in all the years I had lived in that town, the old Economy cemetery had housed his final resting place.

It was around seven in the morning that I pulled into the gravel pathways of the cemetery. A light rain had fallen the night before, the grass was wet, and light dew lay in the air.

I had seen the photo online of the gravesite while looking up other facts. It could have been anywhere. I didn't recognize any landmarks yet something pulled me in the direction of the lower section. My mother's mother was buried there, and we had planted flowers for many years upon her grave.

My eyes scanned the hillside, and I walked along, my feet sopping wet in the open-toe sandals I wore. I was alone, the only sound, the birds chirping their early morning songs. It comforted me.

A disappointing thought struck me though. What if I didn't find him? I walked up and down, to no avail, past row after row of markers and plots.

Frustrated, I retraced my steps to the car, passing my grandmother's grave once again. I had taken a final glance around when I saw it.

There, in perfect dark, chiseled letters was his last name: *Chiccerelli*. My heart pounded in my chest, my steps slowed, and I felt reverence and awe as I stood before his grave. *Pietro and Adelina Chiccerelli.* I dropped to my knees, not minding the wetness as it spread through my light summer pants. I touched the face of the gray marble stone, overcome by emotion, running my fingers over and over their names. Tears rolled down my face. I had found him.

~*~

It had been weeks since I sat in the warmth and familiarity of my mother's house first learning about my great-grandpa.

Usually Mom and I sit back, steaming mugs of coffee in our hands, some sweet crumpet or treat on the table before us. We recant stories, so many stories of our lives. Mom is seventy now, her mind beginning to wander a bit. But here, in my mother's kitchen, we are both young again, revisiting pasts that are long gone. We are both eager and willing to share, laugh and cry over the stories that have touched our lives.

Little did I know that it would be here, new tears would be shed, when worry and gut-wrenching fear would try to overtake me. Here, where I'd face some of the biggest trials of my life.

CHAPTER 2

Terry's Gift

October, 2000

Autumn leaves crunched underfoot on the crisp, October day. Dad was in the front yard raking, a tattered baseball cap perched crookedly atop his head. He stopped when he saw me approaching, and a warm smile broke out on the older, but still handsome face.

"Hey, Kate," he said. I walked over to him and pecked a quick kiss on his cheek. He smelled faintly of Old Spice mixed with sweat, a combination which brought a quick lump to my throat, nostalgic in its wake.

"Your mums look amazing this year, Dad," I said,

observing the colorful rows of crimson, gold, and lavender flowers adorning the walkway to the house.

"I don't think they're nearly as nice as last year," he said, removing his hat and scratching his head.

I held several binders under my arm filled with the printed version of my latest manuscript, "Pietro's Song." I had finally gotten to the point where I had polished it enough times and was ready to submit it to several magazines for publication. My mother was a great help to me when I researched the facts about my great-grandfather. I wanted to show her the finished copy.

"Mom inside?" I asked, even though I knew she was. It was Saturday, and she'd be in her kitchen, baking sheets, utensils and wooden spoons strewn all about her counters.

"Yep, she is, honey," Dad answered. He stood with the rake in his hands, leaning on it for support. He looked a little more tired than usual to me.

"You feeling okay, Dad?" I asked. "Would you like me to help you?"

Dad shook his head. "No, Kate, if it wasn't for our darn trees dropping these leaves every year, I wouldn't have any form of exercise at my age." He chuckled and resumed raking. I touched his arm lightly as I walked away. It appeared Dad still enjoyed a lovely fall day, and the exhilaration of combing colorful piles of leaves together.

Since I had moved to Monroeville, an hour away, I was fortunate my brother Matthew lived close by. He checked in on our folks several times a week and usually did most of the grass cutting and heavier work for them.

Matthew was ten years my junior, a "change of life" baby for my parents. I had been an only child and he had been a welcome, but surprising addition to our family. Even though we were far apart in age, we had always gotten along well.

"Well, okay," I said, calling back over my shoulder and opening the front door of their house. "Just don't work too hard, Dad."

I entered the home of my parents, Ray and Ellen Martino, the scent of pumpkin, and apples in the air. I looked around at couches and chairs, so worn with age, some of the fluff poked through. A wooden crucifix with curled up palm branches behind it hung on one wall, and a huge painting of the hills of Italy in a gaudy ornate frame on another. Floral lamps which had to be from the seventies sat on top of dusty mahogany end tables, and a cream and gold statue of a Roman lady stood in one corner. My heart tugged as I thought of the many happy times in this very room, holidays, warmth, laughter. There weren't many changes from days past and my parents liked it that way.

We had moved to this house when I was ten years old, leaving behind the bustling downtown area of Ambridge.

It was a dream of my mother's to move into a quieter, wooded area. So Dad picked us up and brought us to "the heights" of Ambridge, not completely rural, but enough of a change for Mom. The stillness during the day, although wonderful, was hardest to get used to. I could walk in the middle of the road without fear of being run down, and hardly passed another soul.

It had been tricky at first adapting to the local wildlife, raccoons stealing from garbage cans nightly, owls hooting in the distance, but the musical melody of birds, the feathered angels, was a welcome sound missing from my younger years.

My parent's cat, Lynxy, snaked in and out of my legs, breaking my reverie, rubbing his long, white whiskers against me in greeting. I reached down to pet the soft, gray fur and he immediately produced purrs of delight.

Something crashed in the kitchen, and I arrived in time to find Mom cursing over a dropped glass pie plate. Shards of it had scattered all over the floor, and she shook her hand as if it was hurt.

"What happened?" I asked, walking carefully over the fine pieces of glass glistening in the morning sunshine.

"I'm getting old and clumsy," was Mom's answer. "My hands don't work like they used to."

She was dressed in white cotton pajamas, a thin, flannel housecoat draped over her back, her hair up in rollers. My mother's age had snuck up like a thief, stealing her youth, and offering arthritis with tendrils of pain instead.

"I'll clean it up, Mom," I said, heading for the broom and dustpan that lay in the laundry room beyond her kitchen. Luckily the pie plate had been empty.

I scraped tinkling pieces into the dustpan, depositing them in her trash. When I turned back, Mom was already pulling out other pie pans, metal ones this time from a cupboard above her head. The shelves were practically sagging from all the bowls and baking ware she had accumulated over the years.

"Here, let me do that," I said, gently nudging her out of the way. "I told you to wait for me this morning." An old recipe book from a local church lay atop her kitchen table, propped open with a Disney snow globe. The pages were so encrusted with spills of dried batter, it felt as if you could just pop one of them into the oven and bake it. I chuckled to myself.

"What's so funny?" Mom asked, picking up her favorite paring knife and slicing apples onto an already rolled out crust. Bowls of canned pumpkin, condensed milk, and spices sat close by. A huge bag of McIntosh apples lay open, several apples spilled onto the counter. This was Mom's fall ritual. There was nothing my father and brother liked more than pumpkin pie, but Mom and I were the apple lovers. In order to please all of us, once a year, Mom made both.

"Oh, nothing," I said, and then changed the subject. "I brought you the work I did on your grandfather." I slipped the red apron over my head, the one I always used when helping Mom, and pushed up my sleeves. She looked over to me then and smiled. I knew it would please her; we had both worked so hard learning facts about his life. Mom had supplied me with the beginning of the story; I just filled in the rest.

"Do you think someone will publish it?" Mom asked, her blue eyes twinkling.

I didn't know. I was editing at a local paper, but writing my own stories, which had been a secret passion of mine, left a little to be desired. Or so I thought.

"We'll see, won't we?" I said, rolling out one of the balls of dough Mom already had made. The floured board, the same one that had been my *Nonna's*, an old heavy wooden thing with so many nicks and scratches had been used lovingly many times. I plopped the dough over on its other side, dusting it with a pinch of flour.

"It's such a pretty day," Mom said, that faraway look in her eyes, the one I knew so well before one of her stories was about to emerge. "I love autumn the best of all the seasons." She pulled the first of the finished apple pies from the oven, and the heavenly aroma made my mouth water.

"You *know* it's my favorite season," I said. "Halloween is a few days away, and I still get excited for it." I fluted the edges of the rolled out pastry crust after laying it carefully in one of the pie plates, then pricked it with the tines of a small fork.

Halloween was always a big deal in our family. Years ago, this house was the most decorated and scariest one on the block. My brother and I would begin weeks before, stretching filaments of fake spider web across the porch, cutting Styrofoam into grave stones, painting them to look like the real thing. Then the fun would really begin. We made realistic looking dummies out of Dad's old work clothes, gloves and boots. Fake blood dripped from ugly masks and gnarled rubber hands. Plastic rats, their long tails coiled about their bodies, perched atop cemetery plots, skeletal limbs scattered about.

My brother and I always dressed in elaborately planned costumes whichever movie theme was most popular at the time.

Eerie music and glowing lights completed the look, and many times we'd have to unmask because small children wouldn't approach our walkway to retrieve their candy. It was all in good fun.

My parents were too old now to care, and only one lonely pumpkin sat on a small bench on their porch, with one silly-looking scarecrow standing off to the side.

My mind wandered to an autumn long past. Sometimes there were real haunted houses, not just the make-believe ones of Halloween. Some houses had very real issues going on behind their doors.

Thinking back to the most frightening Halloween of my young life, I began today's tale...

~*~

The year was 1969. Katie Martino, nine years old and her best friends in the world, Carol Garbinsky, Diane Nelson, and the only boy in the neighborhood, Tony Prichard, tagged one another, "You're it!" then ran to the safety of the telephone pole, the "base" where no one could touch you. They had invented a hide-and-seek sort of game out of the usual "It tag."

Growing up on the main drag of Duss Avenue in the small steel town of Ambridge, Pennsylvania had its challenges. A busy thoroughfare, cars and trucks sped by at all hours. There were no playgrounds nearby to play in and the closely- packed homes had only small patches of grass as their front yards, and sometimes even tinier, weedy patches in the back. Cement sidewalks ran the length around their blocks, faded hopscotch in chalky pinks and yellows. The children learned to use their imaginations in the small, cramped quarters, and there was never a lack of things to do, or mischief to get into.

A steel town was an interesting place for kids and like all small towns, had their secrets.

Halloween and autumn hung in the air with the smell of wood smoke, tart apples, and dried leaves. The days were getting shorter, the streetlights coming on long before the children wanted to say goodnight to one another. Nighttime had a slight nip to the air, and sweaters came out of last winter's storage.

This Halloween would be extra special for Katie. Dad had promised he'd think about letting her go out alone with her friends for trick or treats.

Mom always made such a big deal out of Halloween. Every year she would begin planning Katie's wardrobe weeks in advance even though the local five and dime had shelves stocked full of costumes, princesses, pirates, and super heroes. She could have been any of these, but Mom insisted on elaborate, hand-sewn items, cleverly put together.

"What're you gonna be for Halloween this year?" Tony asked Katie, as he huffed and puffed running alongside her before scrambling into the bushes to hide from Carol.

"I'm going to be a fortune teller," Katie called back

over her shoulder, and quickly ducked into a small alley behind some trash cans. She counted to twenty when she heard Carol's voice calling in the distance.

"Okay, I give up guys. Where are you?" Carol screamed out.

Katie emerged first, dusting dirt from her dungarees. Diane and Tony gave up their hiding spots, coming from opposite directions.

"This game's boring," Tony said, approaching the girls. "We need to find something else."

Diane, the tomboy of the group, and one year older, agreed. "Let's ride bikes," she offered. "My parents got me a new one, and I'm dying to try it out. It's supposed be the fastest bike ever."

"Yeah," Tony said, rubbing his hands together with his best mad-scientist impersonation. "Then we can ride past the Gardner place and see which one of us will be the brave one today."

"So, what are the rest of you gonna be for Halloween?" Tony asked. They were standing in front of Katie's house and he picked at the hedge bush in the yard, flinging bits of greenery at the girls. "Katie's gonna be a fortune teller," he crooned and stuck his tongue out at her. "I'm gonna be an astronaut, Neil Armstrong," he proudly stated.

"That's boring," Carol chimed in. "I'm too old for all this 'Halloween stuff' anyway," she said. "My parents want me to hand candy out this year." Her voice had a steel edge to it.

Katie looked at her friend, feeling badly for her. Carol's parents were odd. They seemed to want her to age before her time. She never played with dolls, and her mother made her do chores like a grown up. *I'm glad my parents aren't like that.*

"Yeah, it's baby stuff," Carol said, kicking at a rock with her toe.

"Don't you still *want* to go with us, though?" Katie asked. "We've got the rest of our lives to hand out stupid candy. Your parents shouldn't force you to stay home."

Carol's face darkened, and she took off running from the group. Her house was down the block a little way, and she disappeared into her front door with a bang.

"Ha, ha," Tony laughed. "You made her mad again, Katie. When're you gonna learn?"

Katie looked down the street after her friend. The house was closed up tightly like a fist. It struck her as odd that none of them were ever invited there, and they never played in front of her house.

"Go get your bike, Katie," Diane said. "I'll be back in a few minutes with mine."

~*~

"I dare you," Tony said, whizzing past Katie on his Schwinn Stingray for at least the tenth time. "Just run up and knock on the stupid door. You're such a chicken, Katie. I've done it a zillion times."

Katie sat upon the blue sparkled banana seat, the one her daddy had recently put on her bike. Deep scooped handlebars with blue and white streamers dangled from the ends. "Leave me alone, Tony," she said, flying past the place Tony had referred to, barely glancing at it.

The dark, creepy insulbrick house stood off to the right, its' weeds waist high, and hedges surrounding it like sentinels. The shutters were drawn and no furniture adorned the front porch. The sagging roof, in need of a few shingles, had a chimney that leaned to the right at a crooked angle. No cars were ever parked nearby. Nobody ever saw a soul walk in or out of the place.

Tales had gone around the neighborhood that a crazy man lived there, so deranged, so ugly, his elderly mama wouldn't let him leave the house in the daytime. Gardner was the last name, but other than that, nobody knew much else. The neighborhood children would play silly games, seeing who would be brave enough to knock on the door and run. Other times they would wait until after dark, sneaking around the back of the house to catch a possible glimpse of the madman that lived there and supposedly roamed at night.

Some evenings, in the darkness of her bedroom, Katie peered out the window, the one that faced the back of the Gardner home. She pretended she'd see someone come out onto the back porch, maybe howl at the moon or turn into a bat. At other times, though, she would obsess over the poor, tortured soul who never showed his face. She felt sorry for someone so lonely and wished somehow she could befriend him.

"I'll go knock on the door then," Tony said, a mischievous grin on his face. "It's not like anyone's gonna answer." It was getting a bit darker now, the sun going down quickly, thunder rumbled in the distance and a light, misty rain began to fall.

Diane dismounted her shiny, new bike, and stood beside it. "Go ahead Tony," she said. "Show Katie it's no big deal."

"Come on, guys," Katie said. "We'd better be getting home." Katie didn't want to bother the people who lived there. As frightening as the house looked, her mother had always said that everyone had a story. Who knew what might be going on inside?

"Baby," Tony taunted. "Katie's scared," he said, while propping his kickstand up, and approaching the steps to the drooping front porch.

Thunder crashed overhead, and Tony abandoned his plan.

"Ha, ha," Katie laughed. "Who's scared now?" But she shivered a bit, staring at the darkened windows before her. She could have sworn she saw a blind lift ever so slightly.

~*~

The next morning Katie buttoned up her jacket, picked her book bag from the chair in the living room, and kissed Mom quickly on the cheek. Diane was waiting for her outside and they walked the short distance to Carol's house. Usually standing on the porch, she was nowhere to be seen. The girls stood there a few minutes.

"We're gonna be late for school," Diane said, hefting

her books higher in her arms. "What's taking her so long?"

A scarecrow thin woman, apparently Carol's mother, opened the front door a crack and whispered in a barely audible voice, "Carol's sick today." She closed the door quickly. Raised voices punctuated the morning silence from inside the house. Even with the windows and doors shut, someone was screaming loudly from the sound of it, a man's voice, barking harshly.

Katie flinched, looking at Diane for answers. "Come on, let's go," Diane said, shrugging her shoulders.

~*~

It bothered Katie all day. Even at recess, when the others were playing dodge ball on the playground, she sat off to the side, wondering about Carol. What was it she'd heard this morning?

Carol lived alone with her mother and father. She had two older brothers who moved away years ago. Katie saw Mr. Garbinsky, Carol's father, on several occasions walking home from the steel mill disheveled and irritated, a scary-looking man. He kept his head down and didn't speak to a soul as he passed their home. When Katie called Carol's house to talk with her friend, if her father answered, he would growl angrily into the phone and hang up on her.

Katie asked her dad about him, but Daddy would always shrug it off and say things like, "Don't worry your pretty little self about that man, honey."

It was hard to concentrate in the afternoon and several times one of the nuns smacked her desk with a ruler, bringing her out of the reverie. At the end of the day, when she met Diane, it still nagged at her.

"I have some homework from arithmetic class for Carol," Katie said. "I'm going to bring it to her." She hitched the book bag higher on her shoulder.

"Oh my," Diane said. "You sure are brave going into *her* house." Diane shivered. "Did you know her dad is mean to her mother?" Diane had a smug look on her face as if this type of top secret knowledge made her very important. "Oh yeah, my dad works with him. Says he doesn't talk to anyone much, but overheard him bragging one day about hitting the missus."

Katie looked over at her friend, horrified. The thought of anyone hitting a woman was too much for her. Her own dad was so kind and gentle. The best man she knew.

"Don't say anything to anyone," Diane said in a

hushed voice. "I wouldn't want to get Carol in trouble."

A chilly wind, the icy fingers of a beckoning winter blew as the girls walked along. The skies hung low and gray when Katie walked up the steps to the Garbinsky home.

"Go ahead, Diane. I'll see you in the morning."

"Are you sure, Katie?" Diane looked concerned.

"It's okay," Katie answered, and knocked lightly at the front door.

After rapping several times, the door opened a tiny crack. Carol's face was half -visible and her eye widened in surprise.

"Hey," Katie tried to sound cheerful. "Hope you're feeling better. I brought you some homework so you won't be behind tomorrow."

The door opened just a bit farther. Carol's hand snaked out to grab the papers. She was already closing the door when a voice whispered from inside, "Who is it?"

The stick thin woman from the morning opened the door wider and a ghost of a smile touched her lips. Wonderful smells emanated from inside the home, some type of home baked bread or muffins.

"You're Kate, right?" Mrs. Garbinsky asked, unable to

meet Katie's eyes.

"Yes, ma'am," Katie answered. "Nice to meet you." She put out her hand as her parents had instructed her to do.

A tiny, cold hand shook Katie's. "Would you like to come in for some banana bread?" The woman spoke so quietly it was hard to hear her.

"I'd love that," Katie said. "Would you mind if I called my mom though to let her know where I am?"

Mrs. Garbinsky led her to a telephone on a stand in the dark hallway. Katie looked around at the décor of her friend's home. Pretty glass figurines adorned shelves between stacks and stacks of neatly piled old books. Aside from the dim lighting, it appeared Carol's home was rather warm and inviting.

Carol showed her friend to the kitchen, pulling out a chair for her, while her mother took the heavenly-smelling bread from the oven. Carol and her mother spoke in hushed tones, and it was apparent they were trying to be extremely quiet.

"Father's sleeping," Carol indicated toward the stairs, almost like she'd read Katie's mind. Mrs. Garbinsky sliced into the bread, laying a pat of butter off to the side of the dish she put in front of Katie.

It struck Katie as odd, the fact her friend called her dad, "father". It sounded stiff and formal.

An hour quickly passed, Mrs. Garbinsky apparently so happy to have someone to talk with, she made Katie promise to return sometime. Even Carol seemed to relax as their conversation had gone on.

That night, Kate asked her mother about the Garbinsky family. Mom knew nothing about the strange, quiet family and told Katie the usual: Everyone has a story.

Katie switched tactics and tried prying facts from her mother about the Gardners who lived behind them. Was their son really so ugly and crazy to boot? Mom told her to mind her own business and stop fretting over the neighbors. "Remember," Mom said again. "Everyone has a story."

That night, as Katie lay in her bed unable to sleep, she imagined becoming friends with the strange man inside the Gardner home. What would it be like? *Hello there, sir, I'm Katie. Mind if I sit and chat with you for a bit? Yes, that's right, I won't hurt you.*

She stared into the darkness. There probably wasn't

anyone really living in that house anyway.

~*~

Halloween was just two days away. Katie tried her homemade costume on for at least the tenth time. The flowing patchwork skirt, and peasant blouse was perfect. She had a turquoise bandana to tie upon her head, large dangling hoop earrings, and an armful of colorful bangles. She would be the gypsy queen for a night. Katie pranced and flounced in front of her mirror talking with a strange foreign accent.

She looked up to see Dad standing in the doorway, a camera ready in his hands. Just at the right moment, he flashed a picture of his little girl. Katie took a graceful bow, breaking into a fit of giggles.

"Dad," she said, serious now. "Are you going to let me go out alone for trick or treat this year with my friends? I am nine, you know." She batted her eyes at him. "Tony will be with me and Diane. I promise not to go too far."

Her father appeared to be in deep thought. The camera dangled in one hand, while he stroked his chin with his other. "Well, we'll have to see, won't we?" he said. "I think you could go to most of the nearby streets with your friends if it's alright with your mom, that is."

Katie ran over to her dad, giving him a big hug. "Thank you, Daddy, oh thank you. I feel so grown up."

~*~

The wind picked up a bit on Halloween night. It was six p.m. Pumpkins glowed on porches, the sweet smell of candles inside them. Porch lights came on one by one, and a light drizzle began to fall.

Katie pouted on her front porch. Why did it have to rain tonight?

Diane approached, dressed as an Indian Princess, with Tony tagging along behind in his astronaut gear. Just seeing her best friends in the world, Katie's spirits lifted. Who cared if the weather wasn't perfect? They were going to have fun tonight! The best part, it would be their first time alone without any parents to supervise. Each of them had gotten dire warnings from mothers and fathers. Don't go near strangers. Only go to houses you know. Don't eat any candy until it's brought home and gone over.

Other children were already milling about, ghosts, goblins, witches, fairy queens. They came with their pillow cases ready to be filled with treats, oh so many treats.

Katie and her little group struck off, while she stole a glance down to Carol's home.

~*~

House after house, Katie, Diane, and Tony trudged up long walkways, and steep stairs. After an hour into the night, Diane said she was tired. They neared her house and saw Mrs. Nelson sitting on the porch, a basket of Hershey bars and Mallow Cups on her lap.

"Hey, Mom." Diane said. "I think I have enough candy, so I'll stay and help you now." She sat down with her mother, removed the Indian headdress, stretched out her long legs, and kicked her moccasins off.

Mrs. Nelson tossed a few candy bars into Katie and Tony's bags. They waved goodbye and started off down the block.

"Wow, we got a ton of stuff," Tony said. He held up his bulging sack of treats. In his other arm he carried his space helmet which had been off most of the night.

"Mmm, I know," Katie said. "I can't wait to spill mine out. Of course my dad will pick through and steal his favorite candy first."

They were nearing Tony's house now. "You gonna be

okay?" Tony asked. "I mean, walking the rest of the way to your house, or you want me to walk you there?" He kicked at the ground with his foot.

"Oh my goodness, Tony. It's only around the block. No big deal. There's a lot of people still out. I'm not scared. See you in school on Monday."

Katie walked away, not realizing which direction she was pointed in. The Gardner home stood off to the right, its pointy shrubbery swaying lightly in the wind. Out of the corner of her eye, Katie realized the porch light was on. She would have missed it if she had gone the other way.

Nobody was on the porch; no kids were walking up to knock on the door. There was a single candle burning in a small ceramic pumpkin at the top of the stairs. Katie gulped. Would she be brave enough to walk up to the door? Would her curiosity win and she'd get her wish tonight? Decisions, decisions.

She noticed other families walking across the street. She looked at her watch. Seven forty five. Halloween would be over in fifteen minutes.

With heart hammering in her chest, mustering all her courage, Katie began mounting the crumbling cement stairs to the Gardner porch. The door and windows looked sealed securely, like the entrance to a tomb. She didn't think anyone would really come to the door.

There was no doorbell, so she rapped lightly upon the outside wooden door frame. Nothing. Katie knocked again ever so lightly and waited. As she was about to give up and turned to walk away, the door creaked open and a wizened old face smiled toothlessly at her. The woman was bent over from age, her gnarled fingers wrapped around a bowl filled with candy. The door opened wider, and a youngish man, probably in his twenties, stood next to the old lady. He was heavyset, and pasty white skin filled with freckles covered his face. His mouth drooped at an odd angle. Blue eyes stared out at Katie, and a wide smile broke out onto his homely face.

"Go ahead, Terry," the old woman said. "Give the young lady some candy."

The young man scooped his chubby hands into the dish, pouring several large candy bars into Katie's treat bag. She could hardly breathe and wondered if she was dreaming.

His grin widened, and he said "Happy Halloween" in a voice which sounded like a child's.

"Thank you, honey," the old lady said, more to Katie than to her son. "I wanted my boy to see the kids on Halloween night. It's been a long time since he's been outside, he was pretty sick there for a while. You're the only one who came tonight, bless you, young lady." A tear fell from the corner of the crinkled eyes. She put a trembling hand out to Katie.

"I'm Elsie Gardner," the woman said. "This is Terry, my son." Again, the biggest smile filled the young man's face, eyes dreamy and faraway. Katie shook his hand, thanking him for the candy.

"Well, happy tricks or treats to you," the woman said to Katie, as the door began to close.

Katie walked down the steps in a daze. They'd never believe it. Tony, Diane and Carol would never believe she'd been there. She glanced back in the direction of Tony's house, but it was locked up for the night. As Katie walked the rest of the way home, swinging her bag of candy, her step felt light and her heart glad. Mom was right, there were stories going on behind closed doors. Some you may never know. But tonight she'd gotten a glimpse into the life of a man who would never be "normal" whatever that was. Never again would she look at the Gardner house the same way. They were just people after all. Like her, Mom, Dad, Tony, Diane and Carol.

Katie's house was in view. She seemed to be the only one out this late. As she neared her next door neighbor's house, a man stepped out of the bushes. It was Mr. Garbinsky. He had startled her, and she took a wide berth around him. It was then she noticed him staggering and cursing under his breath. His hand reached out to grab at her skirt, and Katie screamed.

He pulled her roughly toward him, his breath smelling strongly of alcohol. Katie tried to scream again, and found she had no voice. His rough whiskers scratched against her cheek as he bent to her face. In a blind panic, Katie tried kicking his shins, and wriggled to break free of his grasp. He held on tightly to her, words emanating from his mouth that Katie had never heard before.

Just as Katie felt surely she'd pass out, another man approached, yanking Mr. Garbinsky off Katie. He shoved the man roughly, and Katie almost fell with him as Mr. Garbinsky tumbled to the ground. She looked up into the face of Terry Gardner, the young man she had met only moments before. He motioned for her to run, and kicked

Mr. Garbinsky in the ribs with his workman's boots. "Call cops," he murmured in that childlike voice of his.

Katie ran as fast as she could, forgetting all about her bag of treats. Mom was waiting at the door, and her expression changed to panic as she saw her daughter's face and torn skirt.

"My goodness, Katie, what happened, Honey?" Mom grabbed her tightly, hugging her.

"A-a man jumped out of the bushes, Mama." Katie scarcely could breathe and she started to shake. "I- I ran as fast as I could." She was crying now.

"Ray!" Mom screamed. "Ray, someone's been after Katie."

Dad ran into the room, a sick look on his face. A look of regret and pain.

"Call the police, Ray," Mom said, cradling the sobbing Katie in her arms.

~*~

"Young lady," the cop with the kindly face said. "Would you please tell me what happened?"

Katie sat at the kitchen table with her mother's warm, crocheted afghan pulled tightly about her, a cup of hot cocoa before her. Mom and Dad sat on either side of her, while Dad said over and over, "I never should have let her go alone."

Katie didn't want to tell on Mr. Garbinsky. Apparently when the cops checked the spot near the next door neighbor's house, he was already gone. What would happen to her friend's father if Katie told? What would happen to Carol and their precarious friendship? Yet she knew in her heart, lying was wrong.

The biggest surprise was her backward hero. Had Terry Gardner really come to her rescue, like something out of a movie or book? Nobody would believe her, not even her parents.

"I-I'm not sure," Katie said. "It w-was a strange man. I never saw him before," she lied.

"There's a lot of crazies out on Halloween," the cop said, scratching some notes into his note pad. "Probably not anyone local." He looked into Katie's eyes. "Are you sure, young lady?"

Katie nodded, holding onto her hot chocolate with both hands, not looking up at the policeman.

~*~

On Monday morning, Katie told her parents she didn't feel well and would they mind if she missed school? She didn't think she could face Carol.

It had been a strange weekend. Mom and Dad questioned her over and over yet she wouldn't say much about what had happened Halloween night. What should she do about it all? She sat on the edge of her bed and said a little prayer.

"God, I'm not sure what I did was right. You know the truth, and I feel just awful about lying to my parents. But I don't want to get Carol in trouble, either. Please help me do the right thing." Katie clasped her hands before her, eyes squeezed shut. She shivered thinking of Mr. Garbinsky and his foul-smelling breath. She was suddenly frightened that he might come after her again. Katie crawled back under the covers, hearing her parents talking in hushed tones in their bedroom. Dad would be leaving for work shortly.

A knock sounded at their front door, and Katie sat bolt upright in bed. *It's him....* Don't be ridiculous, her mind told her as she heard her dad's footsteps down the hall.

"Huh, it's the strangest thing," she heard him saying. "Nobody was there, but Katie's Halloween bag was at the doorstep." He walked into Katie's room.

"Honey, this *is* your bag, right?" Dad held it up in one

hand. Katie nodded, but her stomach turned over. "I think someone left it on our porch," Dad mused. He looked thoughtfully at Katie then walked out of the room carrying the bag with him.

Katie lay back down, snuggling under the covers. Terry Gardner must have picked up her precious bag of treats the night she was attacked. Her odd hero had come through for her once again.

All day long, Mom fussed, taking Katie's temperature, giving her ice cream in bed. Katie finally got up and walked into the kitchen, finding her treats neatly stacked on the kitchen table.

"I thought you might want some of these," Mom said, coming over to her, pushing her bangs out of the way with her hand, and caressing Katie's face tenderly.

"But look, here's the strangest thing." Mom motioned to the pile of candy, and sitting on top was a crudely drawn card made of construction paper, colored with red, yellow and orange crayons. On the front of it, someone had drawn a picture of a girl carrying a sack. Her hair looked like the way Katie wore hers. When she opened the card, the words *thank you* were scrawled crookedly in black crayon.

"Katie, what's this all about?"

Katie smiled. Her new friend had given her the greatest gift anyone could ever give: her safety. And he had shown her that differences in people weren't so bad after all.

She told Mom about the Gardner home then. She told her about Halloween night and how she met the scary man who lived there. How he had been the one who helped her.

Katie also told her parents the truth about Carol's father. Cops came to the Garbinsky home, and took him away to a rehabilitation facility for a time. Katie lost one friend, but knew she had gained another.

She would see Terry Gardner a few times after that. Katie told the neighborhood kids he wasn't the creepy ghoul everyone had imagined. He became a sort-of legend in their town. Children stopped tormenting him and he began to come out onto his porch as they rode their bikes. His crooked smile and homely face didn't scare them any longer.

Small steel towns have their secrets. And sometimes they are wrapped up in the strangest of packages masquerading as friends.

~*~

Mom sat there, her plate practically licked clean of the apple pie before her. I refreshed her coffee, pouring the steaming liquid into her mug, topping it off with half- and -half just the way she liked it.

I knew it wasn't a tale she liked reliving. It had been such a terrifying time in my young life. Mom and Dad hadn't let me out of their sight for the longest time after it happened. But the fear passed, as things do, and our lives went back to normal. We moved away, not long after into a different, safer section of town, and made new friends.

I didn't see Terry at all after we'd gone, and thought less and less of him as the years progressed. I ran into an old neighbor a few years back and she told me his mother had passed away and Terry was placed into some type of special needs home. She thought he had passed on as well.

"Your pie is delicious, Mom." I said, while clearing the table. Mom stood up and walked over to me, hugging me tightly.

"What's that for?" I asked.

"That's for you, Kate," she said. "I'm so glad you're my daughter."

Dad walked in, his work shirt dusty with bits and pieces of dried leaves sticking to it.

"What'd I miss?" he asked.

"Nothing a good piece of pie won't cure," Mom said, setting a plate of warm pumpkin pie before him in his usual spot at the kitchen table.

I left later that day, Tupperware containers filled with both kinds of pies for my husband Steve and son Mark. They were waiting for me to get ready for our own Halloween on this beautiful October day.

CHAPTER 3

Christmas Angel

December, 2000

The first flakes of snow began to fall on the early December morning. A week before Christmas, and winter seemed late this year; it had held its icy fingers off a little longer than usual.

I curled up on my couch, a soft, multi-colored afghan pulled around me, one of my angora cats resting peacefully on my lap. The other lay nearby, two green slitted eyes blinking lazily at me. I resigned myself to the fact that today would just be a leisurely day on my sofa. Several of my favorite DVD's lay nearby, ones I had watched many times.

One of my small, artificial Christmas trees glowed in tiny white lights, Victorian ornaments dangling from branches covered in fake snow. The larger tree, in the corner of the room, held a mishmash of decorations from many years past. On one branch, a construction paper snow man my son had made in kindergarten sat watch, his shiny sequin buttons sparkling as the multi-color lights bounced off him. On another, an ornate birdcage with two love birds sitting on a swing, welcoming my husband and me into a new home which dated back several years. Bits and pieces of each of our pasts scattered about the branches. So many memories.

The curtains were open to the day before me, skies gray and overcast. The forecast called for a couple inches of snow, and I pouted over this. I was supposed to help my mother bake Christmas cookies today but snow and my car didn't get along. I drove an old, small Chevy Cavalier, and it didn't do well on slick roads. I had promised Mom days ago that I would be there and I didn't want to disappoint her.

It was a yearly ritual, the baking of the Christmas cookies. Mom could really use my help, but knowing her, she was up early, already starting without me. I picked up my cell phone and dialed her number.

"Hey, Mom, how's it going?" I closed my eyes, wishing I could crawl back into bed and snuggle with a book.

"Hi honey. I was watching the forecast just now. Supposed to only get an inch or so of snow by later today. You still coming out? Got a pot of coffee on just for us."

What could I say? "Yes, of course I'm coming, Mom. I'll be there in about an hour or so." I clicked off my phone and called out to my husband.

"Steve, I think I'm going to Mom's today after all." I gently nudged my cat Bella aside. She was sleeping so soundly, she didn't even stir. Her brother, Rocco perked his head up, watching me.

Steve strolled into the room, still in his flannel Steeler PJ's and yawned. My heart still tugged in my chest at the sight of him. Jet black hair and lean body. He smiled that crooked smile of his at me.

"Do you want me to drive you there, Kate?" He walked over and pulled me gently off the couch wrapping his arms around me.

Such a good man. He would do this, I knew it. Saturday,

his precious day off from teaching, and he would take me to my parents knowing how important it was to me.

"No, you and Mark finish decorating the outside today, okay?" I stole a kiss then, a delicious warm kiss. My husband grabbed me tighter for a moment.

"Hmmm, maybe I *won't* let you go after all," he said, stroking my cheek gently with his hand.

Our son walked into the room. "Hey, it's snowing! *Yipeee!*" He rubbed his eyes sleepily, and then looked over at us. "Gross," he said, making a funny scrunched up face.

Mark was eleven years old, and like any young boy, the sight of our affection caused him to vocalize his feelings at our apparent indiscretion.

I wiggled out of Steve's grasp and grabbed my son, making smooching noises in his ear and kissing his cheeks.

"Yuck, Mom, stop it. Okay, I give up," he said, collapsing onto the Lazy Boy recliner, his long, skinny feet dangling off the side.

"You boys gonna be alright today without me?" I slipped into my scuffed winter boots, which lay next to the couch.

"We'll manage somehow," Steve said, pouncing on Mark and tickling him until he giggled so much he could hardly breathe. "We men folk are a tough, rugged bunch, right buddy?" Steve mussed Mark's wavy hair making it stick up in different directions. "Give me your keys, Kate, I'll clear off your car and warm it up for you," Steve said with one final tickle at our son. He slipped into his corduroy jacket and a pair of old tennis shoes he kept by the side door. "You sure you don't want me to take you?"

I handed him the car keys, weighing the situation. If Steve drove, he'd be stuck there for hours on his day off. He had paperwork to catch up on, and I knew he wanted to string the rest of the pastel twinkle lights around our porch.

Mark would definitely get bored at some point, even though my father amused him with his craft kits and old video games. Dad had kept the old Sega game system which had been my brother Matt's. My father and brother had bonded for hours over Sonic the Hedgehog and Galaga. Now Dad and Mark played those same games.

"No, I'll be okay," I said. I gathered up some of my own bake ware, red apron, holiday CD's, and kissed my men goodbye. I said a little prayer, and then backed out of the driveway.

It was snowing pretty heavily as I entered the tollbooth on the turnpike. I rolled my window down for the ticket and a gust of air swooshed snowflakes into the car, chilling me. Since I had no CD player, I fidgeted with the radio stations, trying to find classical Christmas music instead of the modernized versions of old carols. Steve wanted to install one in my old vehicle, but seriously, I knew old Bessie probably was going to give up the ghost sooner than later, and I didn't want to spend money on something frivolous. The radio was fine.

The drive wasn't nearly as bad as I'd expected. Salt trucks dotted the highway, and most other people drove as cautiously as me. I pulled triumphantly into my parent's driveway within an hour, proud of myself for not missing this special baking day over a few inches of snow.

I walked the sidewalk to their house, wistfully remembering the decorations of holidays past. The front yard had held a large sleigh, fake presents and several plastic reindeer. The porch had been home to a huge, outdoor manger scene. Then Dad would wrap strands and strands of the colorful, old time Christmas lights around every bush in his yard and every window in the front of the house. The big lights nobody used anymore which had been hot to the touch, practically a hazard, but no other lights had compared to their vibrant colors. Now, one small snowman stood sentinel, crooked black hat perched atop his head, carrot nose and button eyes. It made me feel sad thinking about my parent's ages now, and how much effort they had put into the holidays in their younger years. I felt the imminent approach of my own passing of time.

Since my father's heart surgery a few years ago, my brother Matt didn't allow Dad to do much of anything. He scolded him when he caught him shoveling snow, or tinkering with gadgets out in the garage. Dad had felt useless at first, and then he discovered crafts.

I smiled to myself thinking of Dad's new hobbies. He had taken over my brother's old bedroom, cleared it of almost everything, even the bed. Tons of craft items, parts to miniature classic ships, pieces of balsa wood planes, and my father's newest passion, dollhouses, covered all surfaces of the room.

The dollhouses were a bonus for him since they took much longer to build. Dad was obsessed as he lovingly and carefully planned the individual rooms of each small home. He went as far as printing up tiny patterns of wallpaper on the computer, pasting them to the walls and hand crafting small wooden furniture items. Some of these were several stories high, and they took up the whole card table Dad used as his workstation. Mom thought they were a waste of time and swore she was going to get rid of all the "junk" in there. Dad told her to just close the door and not let it bother her.

I tapped the front door with the tip of one snow boot, my arms loaded with the items I'd brought with me. After a few minutes, Dad appeared.

"Well, look who's here," he said, opening the door and taking the baking pans out of my arms. "Ellen," he called out. "It's our daughter." He winked at me.

Mom walked into the room and I had to laugh. She had a bright red sweatshirt with Rudolph the reindeer and his red nose as a large pompon. On her head was a fuzzy pointed Santa Claus hat.

"You like my festive look?" Mom asked. "Your father thought I lost my mind this morning."

"No, I'd have to say you look pretty merry, Mom. Come on, let's get started." I walked into the kitchen, the warm, wonderful kitchen with its old-fashioned appliances and laid the rest of my things down on the table. I noticed Mom didn't have anything ready for our baking projects.

Her freshly perked coffee smelled heavenly, and I poured a cup for each of us.

"So you decided to wait for me for a change?" I couldn't resist a small dig. "No guilt speech, come on, Mom, you're slipping."

"Ah, my hip's killing me today," she said, limping over to the table and sitting down. "Every time the weather changes drastically, it really pains me." She pulled the Santa hat from her head and laid it on the table, sipping her coffee.

There it was again. The inference to her age and all the wonderful nuances it brought on. I didn't like it, none of it. I didn't like worrying over her and Dad and I certainly didn't like thinking of myself as becoming older and all the changes it would bring. I'd heard horror stories of hot flashes in some of my friends, night sweats, throwing covers off in the middle of deep slumber, and being unable to fall back asleep for hours after an episode. No, at forty, I wasn't crazy about this new impending time of life.

Dad walked in just then, and before I had a chance to sit, pulled my arm. "Come here, Kate, I want to show you my latest creation."

"Ray, she's got things to do in here," Mom cranked at him. "Stop bugging her about your stupid dollhouses." Mom's mood was certainly in contrast to her cheerful garb.

Ignoring Mom, I followed Dad into his world of miniatures. My mouth dropped open when I saw the latest Victorian dollhouse. Three stories high, a turret, bay windows, shingled roof, and wraparound porch, it had to be the best one ever.

"Wow, Dad, this is amazing." I walked around it several times taking in the detail. It wasn't completed yet, but I could see what it would become. Small pieces of furniture lay scattered nearby on the work table, spidery webs of hot glue still stuck to them.

"Look at this, Kate," Dad said, handing me a small fireplace he had painstakingly put together. Tiny real wood logs sat inside of it and a façade of bricks covered the outside.

I marveled over his patience and skill. Now this was something I could feel good about. Dad hadn't let his age get to him. When confronted with limitations, he simply found new endeavors he could pursue with gusto. I wanted to be just like him.

Kissing Dad on the cheek, I stood there a minute longer.

"What was that for?" he asked. A sweet smile lit up the handsome face I knew and loved so well.

"That was for you, Dad. I'm so proud of you."

I rejoined my mother in the kitchen. Her coffee cup sat empty and I poured her another.

"So, what shall we start with today, Mom? Do you want to make pizzelles and lemon knots or something easier first?" I donned the familiar red apron, and without thinking, perched the Santa hat atop my own head. "There, now I'm feeling Christmassy." I fiddled with the CD player, choosing some of the oldies Christmas music first. Dean Martin's voice crooned softly from the speakers. I began to hum along.

Mom and I spent the next five hours putting together our usual array of goodies. As always we made the traditional Italian pastries, but also chocolate chip oatmeal cookies for Mark and sugar cookies for my brother and his girlfriend.

It was six p.m. when I finished washing the last of the bowls and baking sheets, drying them carefully and putting them away. Mom was exhausted, I could see it in her eyes, but we'd had fun.

"You want to stay for dinner, honey?" she asked. "I have a roast in the fridge from last night. I could warm it up for you."

"No thanks, Mom. I really have to head home. The roads are clear, and I don't want another wave of snow to hit. We'll see you for Christmas Eve dinner. And remember, I'm bringing most of it. You take it easy this year. You deserve it." And I kissed the top of her head. After saying my goodbyes to Dad, I left, feeling a wonderful sense of accomplishment.

~*~

Steve's blazer practically sagged to the ground filled with all the presents and containers of food. I had been up since five a.m. on this glorious Christmas Eve, putting together old favorites and some modern foods I knew my husband and son would eat. Two crock- pots and five large Tupperware containers later, we were ready to set out to my parents. We made this journey every year, eating until we felt we'd burst, and then opening presents together. Since there were so many other relatives to visit, this night had remained a special tradition in my family.

Mark's eyes were huge as we entered my parents' home late that afternoon. Their tiny Christmas tree that stood on one end table may have looked scraggly, but the mountain of gifts sitting on the floor beneath it did not. My parents came through again, generous souls to the end.

My brother Matt and his girlfriend Tina arrived a few minutes behind us. Matt was a big guy, almost six feet tall, the giant of our petite, Italian family. Dad joked for many years that Matt had to be the mailman's son. Tina complimented my brother well. A talkative girl with an easy-going attitude and infectious laugh, we all liked her. They had dated for several years now, and I thought it was only a matter of time before they married.

I missed Matt, and was so glad to see him. Our work schedules prohibited us from spending quality time together.

"Hey sis," he said, crushing me in one of his huge bear hugs. "Missed you, little one."

He smelled of Polo cologne, something I always loved, that piney, woodsy scent. Tina hugged me next and we broke into fits of giggles as she whispered what she'd gotten my brother for Christmas.

"Okay, everyone," Mom said, "enough of this hugging and affection and let's head into the dining room and eat. I'm starving." She had the red Christmas sweatshirt on again, and the Santa hat.

Though the dining room was small, Dad had put the extra leaf into the old mahogany table to accommodate all of us. Mom's best Christmas dishes adorned it, sparkling crystal goblets which she only took out this time of the year.

I finished up in the kitchen, reheating some of the foods I'd made earlier and plugged in the crockpots, setting them to high.

We always ate buffet style, but first we gathered at our places around the dining room table, holding hands and bowing our heads. All eyes looked to Mom.

"Father God," she began, "I want to thank you for another year of this family being together. I want to thank you for each and every one of us gathered here tonight. Thank you for our children's safe arrival, the wonderful meal we are about to eat, the love this family has shared through the years and whatever adventures may lay in our futures. We give all praise and glory to you, in your Son's name. Amen."

With that, we lined up in the kitchen and one by one took turns scooping linguini and clams, smelts, haddock, shrimp cocktail and vegetable lasagna, the meatless dishes which made the substance of an Italian family. The chicken cutlets I'd made for my husband and son sat alone in a glass baking dish, and the two heathens proceeded to load their plates with them and side dishes of potatoes and vegetables. Steve didn't care for fish, but it was tradition that Catholics fasted on Christmas Eve. What else could Steve eat? I joked with him for years if he ate meat, he might be facing eternal damnation.

Later, as the men cleared dishes from the table, we girls organized the presents in the living room.

At seven o'clock that night, we began our family ritual. Each person took a turn opening one present at a time. This usually took hours. One by one, we *oohed* and *aaahed*, complimenting one another on such thoughtful gifts. Nobody could outdo my brother though. Matt made mental notes all year long when talking with any of us, and always chose the most amazing, thoughtful items.

He watched our father's face carefully on the last

colorfully wrapped package. Inside was another wrapped box, a little smaller. Through several layers of paper, a thin, rectangular box was finally revealed. Matt leaned in closely. When Dad opened the lid, I saw his eyes open wide in wonder and surprise. He pulled a watch from the box, and lovingly held it in his hands. A tear slipped out of one eye,

"What the heck?" I asked. No present I'd ever gotten Dad had even come close to this type of reaction.

"Do you all know what this is?" Dad asked. After taking turns shaking all our heads, he told us.

"This is a watch I had as a little boy. My older brother got me one just like it when I was ten. It's a Lone Ranger watch. See, it has a picture of the masked man sitting on his trusty steed, Silver." He gazed at it like a lover. "I lost mine when I was a teenager. I never had the heart to tell my brother. It meant so much to him at that time saving up money to get me something so special." Dad's voice trailed off and he sat quietly. Apparently the memories made him feel like a little boy once again.

"Matt, that's awesome," I said. "How do you find this stuff?"

"EBay, Sis," he said. "I've been looking for one for

years."

I watched Mom out of the corner of one eye. She looked tired. I got up to bring in the huge platter of cookies we'd baked together. Offering one to her first, I asked, "Did you have a nice time tonight, Mom? You were a little quieter than usual."

"I was just thinking," she said. "Did I ever tell you all about the Christmas Eve when I was ten? The night we had a special visitor?"

"I don't think so, Mom," I said. Knowing it was time for one of her long, unusual family tales; we settled in and waited for her to begin. . .

~*~

In 1941 times were tough and money was tight. The war had been raging for a little over a year across the ocean. Now it threatened America as well. Families said goodbye to young sons, watching them head overseas one by one, not knowing if they'd ever see them again. FDR was president, radio was king, big band music was in full bloom and the country was finally emerging from the Great Depression.

In the small steel town of Ambridge, Ellen Romano, ten years old, carried her coat and schoolbooks on an unusually warm December day. It had been a little disappointing since snow hadn't fallen yet, and she worried it wouldn't be a white Christmas. With only two weeks to go, it had been such a strange winter.

Ellen walked past the newly- built middle school at the corner of the long hill leading to her street. A few kids stood around outside playfully jabbing at one another, girls flirting with boys and vice versa. Ellen waved to a girl she knew.

She approached her own block, taking her time, all the while watching for signs of her father's car. She breathed a sigh of glorious relief when her house was in view. Papa's old Dodge wasn't anywhere in sight. Maybe he'd work late tonight and they'd have some peace. God knew it had been tough recently. With money so precious and tight, and her father's gambling, they had to make due many times with much less food on their table. And if Papa lost in his card games, and his drinking worsened, he'd take it out on their family. Many nights Ellen lay in bed unable to sleep, fingers plugged in her ears, her father's angry voice bellowing, and the sound of a slap, or of a piece of overturned furniture. Many nights, she held onto her sister, Claire, as they waited for the blessed silence which would finally come. But when Papa finally passed out from drunkenness, the heartbreaking sound of their mother's sobs would begin.

Her mother's careworn face broke into a smile as Ellen walked through the door. Mama had a huge apron tied around herself, flour up to her elbows, and a hair net pulled over her short curly permanent wave.

"How was school, *cara mia?*" Mom asked. "What did you learn?" Ellen pulled a chair from under the kitchen table and sat looking at her mother. Her brother and sister weren't home from high school just yet. This was precious one on one time with Mama.

"Oh, Mama, I learned how to multiply numbers today. I'm getting so good at it," Ellen said reaching for a small pinch of her mother's dough and making a little ball with it.

"That's good then," Mama said. "I didn't have the opportunities you do when I was your age. I had to quit school to help take care of my brothers and sisters. You kids are so fortunate today." Mama plopped a huge slab of dough onto her floured board. "I'm trying to get some ciambelles made for Christmas Eve dinner at Aunt Angie's house. You know how much your Papa loves them."

Ellen groaned inwardly. Papa was coming to Christmas Eve dinner then. He had missed several years in a row, preferring to spend the special night playing cards with a bunch of other drunken men down at the local S.O.I. club. He hadn't had the decency to show up for their dinners before. No matter. Christmas Eve was such a warm, wonderful night. So many of her cousins, aunts and uncles would be there, gathered at Aunt Angie's house. There would be laughter, stories, games, and a small gift stocking for each small child filled with an apple, orange or some type of fruit, nuts or maybe even a small trinket. Oh, Ellen couldn't wait.

~*~

A few days before Christmas Eve, it hit. One of the biggest snowstorms ever. With it being an unusually balmy winter, the snow was a complete surprise and Ellen awoke to the brightness of the morning, huge, fat flakes cascading outside her window. She jumped up in the flannel nightgown she wore, running over to the window, wiping at the frosty pane with her sleeve for a better view.

Her sister Claire rolled over in bed, clucking her tongue in anger. "What's wrong with you, little girl? We have at least another hour to sleep." Claire pulled the bed covers over her head and sighed.

"It's here, Claire! The snow has finally come! Oh, I'm so happy," Ellen said, doing a little dance around the room.

"You won't be so happy when you wake Papa up," Claire mumbled from under the covers. "He was up pretty late last night. Hush up."

Nothing could stop her glee at this moment. Not even her father.

A little later, Ellen and her sister sat in their tiny kitchen eating bowls of Cream of Wheat. Mama was a little quieter than usual. She had dark circles under her eyes and her hands shook as she served her girls.

"What's wrong, Mama? Where's Tony?" Ellen asked, referring to her older brother.

At that, she saw Mama's face grow pale. "*Shhh*, quiet, young one," Mama said. "Your brother got in big trouble last night. I let him sleep in today."

Apparently, Tony had gone out late with his friends. He was sixteen years old, and turning into a regular night owl. He and the boys played cards sometimes at each other's houses. But last night, he hadn't been home by his usual curfew of ten p.m. Papa sat up waiting for him and when Tony strolled in at midnight with the smell of whiskey on his breath; their father had almost killed him. He had beat Tony with his belt, while Mama tried to intervene. It had been no use, and when Papa was done, Tony defiantly looked at him and said, "See, now I'm just like you." Their father had gone to bed then, apparently exhausted from his murderous rage.

"So you see, girls," Mama said. "It's not such a good day for me. My dear son, my poor boy."

Ellen got up from her place at the table and hugged her mother. Mama, always a little embarrassed by the show of affection, brushed her away.

"Now girls, go. Have a good day at your schools. When you come home tonight, we'll finish our meal preparations together for Christmas Eve, okay?"

Ellen buttoned up her coat, grabbed her books and looked at her sister. Claire appeared to be lost in her own world. As the girls left, they walked in silence for a while.

"I heard the fight last night," Claire said unable to look at her sister. "I'm so glad you were fast asleep. I don't think you could have taken it, Ellen." Claire pulled her threadbare coat a bit more tightly around herself shivering. "Papa's so mean. I hate him. Sometimes I wish he'd die."

"Oh, Claire, you mustn't say such things. It'll come back on us." Ellen quickly said a prayer and forked her fingers, making the sign against the evil eye at her sister.

Both girls walked on in silence, Ellen kicking up tufts of snow before her.

In school though, Ellen couldn't rid herself of her own bad feelings. *Why? Why did Papa have to be so mean? Her good brother didn't deserve the beating he'd gotten last evening. He was always such a great young man. So what if he messed up one time, didn't their stupid father do that when he was young?*

And what about Mama? She had seen her father on several drunken occasions grab his wife and shake her, while Ellen and her siblings sat cowering in fear. She'd remembered hearing stories of Papa's father, a hostile, bitter man who ruled his wife and children with his hateful fists. Was it any wonder her father could be so unkind then?

God, if you're there, please show me a sign. Show me some type of kindness or let me know you hear me. We can't go on like this. I'm so afraid, God. Please, please help Papa to change.

Later that night, Tony sat at the kitchen table while

Mama was rolling out homemade pasta noodles. He helped her cut the long strands into thin strips. When Ellen walked through the kitchen door, she ran to her brother, squeezing him tightly. And when Papa came home from the steel mill later, he was reserved. There was no talk at the family table during supper, just the scrape of forks against plates in the silence of the kitchen.

~*~

The snow continued into Christmas Eve. At least eight inches lay on the ground, the sparkling diamonds of crusty snow in piles.

Ellen, Claire, Mama and Tony trudged the five blocks to Aunt Angie's house. Papa, the only driver in their family was asleep from working a late night shift and would join them afterward. Each of them carried satchels filled with foods and baked goods Mama had prepared. They wore their warmest winter coats, rubber galoshes and mittens. It was still snowing lightly as they approached Angie's home; beautiful fat flakes with lacy patterns landing on bushes. To Ellen, absolutely nothing could steal her joy on this late afternoon.

Uncle Eddie and Aunt Ida were just arriving when they reached the house, followed by their children, Annie,

Patsy and Bobo. Grandma Adelina leaned heavily on her cane, as Uncle Eddie carefully guided his mother-in-law across the snowy path. "Come, Mama," Eddie said to her, helping her up the porch steps.

Ellen's favorite cousin, Wally, was already in the house when she walked through the door. A regular prankster, nobody could make her laugh the way he did. He was one year older, but so small; people usually mistook him for a young child. Wally was the third of four children, Aunt Angie's favorite. He sneaked behind Ellen when she entered the kitchen with her parcels.

"Boo!" Wally said, laying his hand on Ellen's shoulder. Ellen jumped and screamed, almost dropping the bag of homemade cookies.

"Silly goose," she said. I knew you were there all the time." She went up to other aunts and cousins, handing over all she'd been carrying as Mama and Claire walked in behind her.

There had never been anything like the foods prepared in Aunt Angie's kitchen. Artichokes in olive oil, pasta with tuna sauce, baccala fish, smelts, fried green peppers and roman beans. Ellen's mouth watered as she looked at the feast spread before her. Mama brought struffoli, little dough balls soaked in honey, ciambelles, hard Italian biscuits and a huge bag of wine cookies, flaky on the inside and a bit crispy on the outside. Aunt Ida pulled homemade bread from her own satchel along with soft buns, their outer edges crusty brown. Wine decanters were placed on the table with a small bottle of anisette. It didn't matter none of these people were well-to-do. What mattered on this night, they were rich in their heritage, love of family, and anticipation of the birth of the savior.

"Is Sam coming, Louisa?" Angie asked her sister, after taking her coat and hanging it on the cellar landing.

"Yes, he was sleeping. He should be here before we start to eat." Ellen watched her mother carefully as she said this. Nothing in Mama's face betrayed her emotions. She was stoic to the last, and nobody in the family knew about Papa's drinking and temper.

At six p.m. promptly, the family gathered around the table for the blessing when Papa walked through the door. He made a striking figure, coal black hair, neatly trimmed moustache. If she hadn't been so frightened of him, Ellen would think her papa was one of the most handsome men in town. He took his place at his wife's side, and all were silent for a moment. Uncle Carmen,

Angie's husband, usually a man of very few words, said the blessing.

In Italian, Carmen spoke of God's goodness and bounty. He thanked Him for providing work for all of them, and warm houses, food on the table. He thanked his heavenly father for watching over their sons who fought in the terrible war. He thanked God for his wife and children and all who were gathered together in their home. When he finished, each man held a glass of wine before them, and toasted, "salute" to each other.

Aunt Angie set to work, heaping dishes with steaming foods. By the time the last small child had been served, all eyes looked to the matriarch of the family, Adelina. She smiled her toothless grin, and said the words they all had been waiting for: "*Mangia, tutti!*" Everyone, eat!

Ellen watched her mother out of the corner of one eye as she wolfed down pasta. Mama seemed content, Papa's hand rested atop hers, giving a little squeeze of affection from time to time. Talk was light and fun, each person adding a little something to the conversation as they continued their meal.

Cousin Giorgio brought his accordion out after dinner, while the men retired to the cellar to continue drinking glasses of homemade red wine. The children helped their mama's clear the table, putting away leftovers and helping wash dishes.

Ellen and Wally got the messy job of bagging garbage to bring out to the tin can behind the house. As they put on their coats, a soft knock sounded at the front door. Everyone glanced around at one another, nobody else was expected. Perhaps a neighbor stopping by to wish them goodwill.

"I'll get it, Mama," Wally said, running from the room.

Naturally, Ellen thought, *anything to get out of helping me*. She dropped the bag of garbage she'd collected, following Wally into the living room. Wally opened the front door and there, before the two children on the porch stood a man, shabbily dressed, hardly enough clothing on a night such as this. Old dungarees and work boots, flannel shirt and no coat. A blast of frigid air blew into the room. The man stood there, rubbing his hands together, his rheumy eyes darting between the two children.

The first thing Ellen noticed, besides the strange gentleman, was that it had stopped snowing. In the glow of the streetlamps, the last of the fallen snow glistened under the cast of the lights. The next thing she noticed was not another soul was out. Nobody walking, no neighbors outside their homes.

"Would you kind folks be able to spare me something to eat tonight?" The man's gravelly voice startled Ellen out of her reverie. Had she heard him correctly? Barely enough to feed all of them and he wanted some of it? But on the tail end of that thought, Ellen became ashamed. Poor man looked as if he hadn't had a meal in a long time.

It was Wally who broke the silence. "Come in, sir," he said, motioning for the man to enter. "Wait here." He and Ellen ran to the kitchen, breathless with excitement.

"What's going on?" Angie asked, drying the last of the metal sauce pots.

"Mama, there's a man at the door," Wally said, catching his breath. "He says he's so very hungry and would we have something to spare?"

Ellen stood behind Wally, waiting to see what the grownups would do.

Aunt Angie broke the silence of the moment. "Let me go see him." She walked from the kitchen, her dish towel still clasped in one chubby hand. Ellen and Wally stood close by.

The man stood perfectly still, his eyes almost dreamy in the warmth of the home. He appeared to be whispering something, lost in his own world. Ellen thought he must be feeble or crazy.

"Well hello there," Angie said, walking over to the man. His eyes opened wider and a smile broke out on the homely face. It appeared to light up his countenance, and for a moment, he didn't seem so scary.

"I'm so very sorry to bother you tonight, ma'am," he said in that growly voice. "You see, I'm so terribly hungry. I haven't been home in a while. I just wondered if you perhaps had a little food to spare."

It was then Ellen noticed a change on the man's face, and how blue and piercing his eyes became as he looked directly at her aunt.

Angie began to protest for a moment. "Well, I'm sorry, but we barely have enough for ourselves." She was interrupted by Ellen's mother.

"Nonsense," Louisa said, putting her hand on her sister's arm. "A few of us already packed some things for you." She handed a paper sack to the man, its sides bulging, and the heavenly aroma of the foods pouring from it.

"It's fine, Angie," Mama said. "Please, take it, and have a Merry Christmas."

Ellen's heart burst with pride for her mother, a kind, good woman who would give the last of her own food to another.

"Bless you all," the man said, accepting the parcel and holding it tightly as if they'd change their mind and take it back. "You have no idea how much this means." He turned to go.

Angie walked ahead of him, and began to open the door. An icy blast of wind blew into the room, and Ellen wanted to protest. Couldn't he just stay there with them and eat his meal? Where would he go? Did he have family nearby perhaps?

As if he read her mind, the stranger turned to face Ellen and said the most perplexing thing. "Your prayer has been heard." With that, he walked out the door and into the night.

The women went back to the kitchen. They talked among themselves of the strange man and the odd things he had said. The sound of the accordion rose from the basement with the voices of their men singing.

Ellen and Wally looked at one another. "Wally," Ellen

whispered. "I'm scared. Why do you suppose he spoke to *me* like that? What does it mean?" Her curiosity got the better of her and scared or not, she wanted to see where he was headed. "Let's walk outside and see where he goes. I'm dying to know."

The two children slipped out onto the front porch. It had only been a moment or so since the man had gone. They peered in both directions up and down the block, across the street at the other houses. No sign of him. It was then Wally piped up, his eyes widening, his finger pointing at the ground.

"Look, Ellen," he said. "Would you just look? There isn't a footprint out here, not one. It was snowing earlier, and it stopped when we were eating." Wally's eyes looked about to pop from their sockets.

"I don't understand," Ellen said, shivering a little in the cold. "What do you mean?" Then it dawned on her. There would have been some type of footprints on the porch or the walkway which led to the house. The man had some big laced up boots on his feet, and they would have imprinted in the snow. "What in the world?" Ellen walked off the porch, again looking in every direction. No footprints on the sidewalk either way. It was as if he'd disappeared.

They ran into the house. "Mom!" Wally screamed. "Come here!" Angie, Louisa and Ida came into the living room, questioning him.

"No footprints! He just vanished into the night!" Wally tugged at his mother, hurrying her out onto the front porch.

"Well, I'll be. . ." Angie said.

~*~

Ellen lay in her bed unable to sleep that night. She turned on her side toward Claire and sighed.

"What, baby girl? Why are you so fidgety tonight?" Claire sat up leaning on one elbow.

"Claire, did you notice how extra kind Papa seemed tonight? Even though he'd been drinking with the others, he seemed, somehow . . . different." Ellen flipped the light switch on her bedside table. "I, I prayed about him to God today. I, I think He heard my prayers."

"What do you mean, Ellen?" Claire asked, reaching for her sister's hand.

"I think that ugly man who showed up at Aunt Angie's tonight was an angel, Claire. I think he came to deliver a special message to me."

Claire laughed then. "Nonsense, Ellen, he was a poor lonely soul, looking for a meal. He probably had a wife and children in some dirty apartment nearby and shared his food with them."

"No," Ellen protested, sitting up and pulling her hand away from her sister's touch. "No, it was really an angel. We learned a bible verse in Sunday school one time. Here, it's in my notebook. I'll read it to you."

Ellen got up from bed to retrieve her bible school notebook from the corner desk in their room. She leafed through it under the glow of the bedside lamp. "Here it is, Claire, look."

"Be careful to entertain strangers, for by doing this, some people have entertained angels without knowing it." Ellen shut the notebook. "Don't you see, God answered my prayer. He sent us an angel to test us, and we passed the test. Mama's kindness will be rewarded." Ellen shut the light and whispered in the darkness. "Did you know he said something to me before he walked out the door?" When her sister didn't answer, she continued. "He said your prayer has been heard."

"You're making that up," Claire said. "You shouldn't lie about such things."

"Ask Wally, Claire. He heard it too. I'm telling you, the man disappeared, there wasn't one footprint, and he did say that to me. And Claire, his face . . . changed. He was so scary looking when I first saw him, and when he spoke to Aunt Angie and thanked Mama, his face became almost beautiful."

"You read too many stories and listen to too many radio shows. Get some sleep. We'll talk about it another time." Claire lay back down and turned her back toward her sister. Ellen lay there a while longer, silently giving thanks to God for hearing her prayer. She just knew things were going to get better with her Papa. Why else would God send His messenger to them?

~*~

My mother finished the tale, wiping her eyes with the sleeve of her Christmas sweatshirt. I got up, fished a Kleenex out of the box, and handed it to her. I sat next to her, hugging her tightly. Nobody spoke for a few minutes.

It was then my son piped up. "Gram, did your father really change after that night? What happened?" He sat on the edge of his seat, and it made me feel good knowing he'd listened to her story so carefully and perhaps had been touched by it.

Mom looked up, a smile playing at the corner of her mouth. "Well, yes, he did. It wasn't big changes at first, but little by little we all noticed something different about him. He stopped gambling after that Christmas, which was a pretty big deal for him. I overheard him talking with my mother late into the night after the New Year that he'd had a dream of some sort, a vision perhaps of himself as a lonely, old man without his family. All his money was gone, and we were all gone as well. He said he saw himself in a filthy, roach-infested apartment, cold and scared. I think the dream terrified him, and I have no doubt it was another intervention by my 'angel'. He was much kinder to my mother after that, but he still drank at times though. I guess some things were easier for him to work on than others." Mom reached for the platter of cookies, biting into her ciambelle, the crumbs from the crusty biscuit falling into her lap. She absently brushed them away and sighed.

"I believe you, Gram," Mark said. "I heard that same bible verse in church one time. Wow, you were pretty lucky. I've never had anything that neat happen to me." Mark got up and reached for his favorite cookies, piling them onto a small paper plate I had laid near the platter.

We all sat there content in the company of our loved ones. Mom's story had touched each one of us I could tell. Faraway looks on faces, reverential silence. It was the best Christmas story we'd ever heard.

~*~

At ten minutes to midnight on New Year's Eve, my husband and I sat with our crystal goblets of Asti Spumante near us. The last embers of the fire Steve had built earlier glowed in the darkness, the smell of the wood smoke lightly in the air. The Christmas tree lights twinkled in the dimness. Mark lay on the lazy boy recliner, fast asleep. I thought back to the past year and all that happened. I felt blessed, warm and loved. Steve traced the top of my hand lightly with the tip of one finger.

"What are you thinking about, beautiful?" he asked.

"Just how blessed we are, and how grateful I am for you, Mark and my family."

The ball began to drop on the television set before us, the last numbers of the old year ticking away. Steve raised his glass, clinking it to mine and we took a sip as Auld Lang Syne played in the background. We put our glasses down and kissed long and hard as the new number of the year flashed on the TV, 2001. We'd come through Y2K and all the fear the media had thrown at us surrounding the possible meltdowns and madness that was supposed to happen. 2001, a year filled with promise and hope. I just knew it would be a great one, monumental.

CHAPTER 4

Matthew's Courage

September, 2001

"*Kate*, hello, are you there? I need to speak to you, please, please call me." I arrived home to my brother's frantic voice and the little red light blinking, blinking. I played the message over and over, a feeling of dread growing in the pit of my stomach. My legs, quivery Jell-O, threatened to fold under me.

My son Mark and husband Steve stood next to me, and I tried to appear stoic. I wasn't doing a good job and before my trembling hand could reach out to the answering machine one more time, Steve stopped me and brought me into the living room.

"Sit down, Kate. You don't know anything yet." I felt

my lip quivering and saw my son as he walked into the room, eyes way too big for his face.

"Is Uncle Matt going to be okay, Mom? When will we know something?" He stood there looking at me and I couldn't answer him.

Motherly instinct finally took over and I pushed Steve away, Steve who sat next to me and was holding me in a death grip, arm tightly around my shoulder as if he could ward off all evil from me.

"How are you doing, Bud?" I asked my son, kneeling before him. "Were you scared when you heard?" I smoothed his light brown hair from his eyes, wishing I could erase this day and begin again.

"Yeah, I was in science class when it came over the speakers. Our teacher had a TV in the room, and we sat and watched for a while. I was afraid something would happen at my school." Mark seemed too young and too old to me all of a sudden. A little boy who'd had to witness something horrific, as we all did on this day. A grown up in a tiny body, never to feel quite secure again. How could any of us?

"I just walked into the teacher's lounge," Steve said, "and Mr. Belfiore came running in out of breath to tell us." He pulled me to my feet and the three of us held on to one another. Our little family.

I wanted and yet not wanted to turn the television on and watch the terrifying events unfold even now. It was twelve noon, at least two hours after the last of the news that held our country on edge, mortified. But I had a bigger stake than some of the others. My brother, Matt, had an appointment today you see. An appointment in the South Tower of the World Trade Center.

~*~

Dad ended up in the hospital the first part of 2001. Mom called me one morning while I'd been getting ready for work, and in her inimitable style, told me the ambulance had just arrived to whisk my father away. Never one to panic, Mom remained calm, stoic. I, on the other hand, anxiety-ridden from youth, became hysterical, angry that she hadn't called me sooner.

It had turned out to be irregular heart rhythm, and the cardiologist recommended a Defib Pacemaker for Dad. The surgery hadn't taken very long; Dad was out of the hospital in a day, and feeling completely normal, back to building balsa wood airplanes and dollhouses.

I wished I could be more like Mom, and asked her the

secret to her serenity. "My faith in God," was the answer I received. It made sense. Mom had always been the rock in our family, a pillar of strength when times were tough. She spent the first part of her day with a small prayer book open before her, studying scriptures. I enjoyed church and knew bible stories from my Catholic school upbringing, but wasn't sure where I stood in true matters of faith. God felt unapproachable to me sometimes. A massive Santa Claus who knew when I was good and when I was bad, waiting to pounce and deliver mighty wrath. I prayed sometimes. It was something taught when I was a young girl. But the true, heartfelt meaning of prayer just wasn't a part of my life.

Little did I know how very big prayer would become to me later that year, and how true faith in God and a relationship with His son would affect me.

My brother, Matt, got a new job after Dad's heart surgery, around springtime. Always good with children, Matt became director of an agency he'd been working with for the last three years. He had risen to great heights in a short time not only because of his college background in youth counseling, but Matt was the type to volunteer in as many programs for children as he could.

His girlfriend, Tina, on more than one occasion, would call me and remark over how little she saw of him. What could I say? I was lucky we'd been together at Christmas last year. Except for running into him at our parent's house on occasion, my once a week phone calls with my brother were more precious than ever.

"Hey, Sis," Matt said to me while we chatted by phone on the glorious spring day. "I'm going to ask Tina to marry me this summer." He sounded like a schoolboy with a crush and I could just picture him pacing as we talked.

"It's about time," I teased. "Thought you were going to become an old bachelor. Mom wants more grandkids, you know." I sat with my feet upon my desk in my writing room, rays of bright sunshine filtering from the window behind me. Dust motes sparkled in the air, while my cat Rocco looked sleepily at me from his post at the door. His sister Bella glared from the hallway. When she tried to walk past her apparently sleeping brother, Rocco would bat his furry paw at her, swiping her fluffy tail with his claws. She kept retreating further out into the hall.

"Yeah, I think so too," Matt said. "Tina's been hinting to me for the last year. Can you blame her, this total package she's getting?"

I had to laugh. Matt was not by any standards a cocky man. If anything, he had been extremely shy growing up. His brawny physique and impressive height caused women to turn their heads when he'd walk by. But he never appeared to notice.

"Oh yes, she's so lucky," I teased. "Does she know about your nail biting, your snoring, your..." He interrupted me then.

"Okay, I get the point, Sis. Thanks for reminding me." Matt cleared his throat. "Hey, I got chosen to represent St. Martin's Agency in a big shareholder's meeting this fall."

"Oh, what's that all about?" I asked.

"I guess every few years they nominate someone to go speak to the powers that be about our agency, kind of like begging for funding, etcetera. I'm not the greatest speaker by a long shot, but out of our whole staff, they thought I'd be the best one for it."

"Wow, Matt. I'm proud of you. You've really come far in a short time, Bro." I swung around in my chair to retrieve Bella. Stepping cautiously over her brother, I scooped the fur ball into my arms and cuddled her to my chest. She gave her brother an almost defiant look of triumph. *Ha, see, I'm Mom's favorite.*

"Where is the meeting?"

"It's in New York, this September, I think," Matt said. I heard him shuffling papers on the other end of the phone. "Yeah, here it is, Tuesday, September eleventh. I guess I have to stay a few days and they're putting me up in the big Hilton."

"Are you driving?" I asked. I knew Matt's fear of flying. He'd only gone once when we were younger and my parent's practically had to drug him to get him on the plane.

"No, I have to fly. It'll be okay, I guess. Well, Kate, I gotta run. Tina's calling. Talk to you soon, love you." And he hung up.

I sat there with Bella, stroking her soft, gray fur, the sounds of her purrs in rhythm with my breathing. *I'm happy for you, Matt.* I thought to myself. *If anyone deserves a good life, it's you, brother.*

In July, Mom and I sat at her kitchen table while Dad puttered away in his little room. I could hear him talking to himself every so often. It was one of our usual Saturday get-togethers and we sipped iced tea instead of our usual steaming cups of coffee. Mom had made a pot of her famous chipped ham barbeque, a southwestern Pennsylvania favorite. I always wondered what it was that made it so extra special. I was already on my second sandwich, the tangy sauce dribbling down my chin.

"Kate, what do you think about Matt and Tina?" Mom tapped the table with the fingers of one hand, while the other traced circles around the condensation on the outside of the glass of tea before her. "She's good for him, don't you think?"

"Yes, she definitely is, Mom. I liked her from the start." I finished the rest of my second sandwich, dabbing the sauce from my face.

"Good to the last drop, eh?" Mom asked.

"Sorry, that was kind of gross. Anyway, yeah, we have until next spring to get ready for the wedding. Any ideas?"

"Well, Tina wants us to bake cookies, you know that already. She's going to have a little meeting here at my house with the girls she picked for her bridal party sometime next month. This way we can get some dates for the shower, gown fittings and such." Mom finished the glass of iced tea before her, ice cubes clinking when she set it back down. She rubbed her eyes for a moment, and I thought she might have gotten one of those brain freeze headaches. When she looked back up at me, though, her eyes were red and teary.

"What is it, Mom? What's the matter?"

"I was just thinking back to the time I found out when I was pregnant with your brother." She tore a piece of paper towel and dabbed her eyes with it. "He was such a surprise, such a blessing. I'd always wanted a little boy. Did I ever tell you all the events surrounding my pregnancy?" When I shook my head, she continued.

"I miscarried twice between you and him, Kate. The doctor's didn't think I'd ever have another baby. As a matter of fact, they told me not to. . ."

~*~

"Ray, I don't feel so good," Ellen Martino said to her husband as they watched The Carol Burnett show on an evening in late December. "Must be the darn flu."

Ellen suddenly bolted from the couch and just made it into the bathroom in time. She sat there, feeling achy all over. Wiping her mouth with a washcloth, she stood shakily to her feet. *Yep, must have caught it from the supermarket. Everyone was coughing and sneezing there today.*

Ray stood in the doorway. "You okay, honey?"

"Does it look like I'm okay? No, let me go lie down. I need to get some rest, is all." Ellen brushed past her husband, and headed directly for the bedroom. Katie was in her room, playing with the Lite Brite set she'd gotten for Christmas.

"What's the matter, Mama?" she asked.

"Feeling sick, kiddo. Better not come near tonight. Don't want you getting this bug." Ellen dragged herself into her own room. She climbed into bed and tried laying on her right side first, then turned over on her left. All of a sudden, the room felt as if it was spinning.

Their ranch house was small, and the bathroom was only steps from her bedroom door. Ellen barely made it this time.

"Ellen, do you want me to call a doctor?" Ray stood there, concern etched on his face. "I haven't seen you this sick in a long time."

"No, it'll pass. Maybe I ate something that disagreed. Shouldn't have had those stuffed peppers earlier. Whoa, yuck, don't want to talk about food right now." She got sick once again.

Later that night, totally fatigued, Ellen fell into a fitful sleep. Something nagged at her, but she couldn't place a finger on it.

The next day wasn't much better, and Ellen felt completely drained even though she'd slept at least nine hours. Her daughter, Kate was still off from school until after the New Year, but Ellen couldn't even get out of bed to make breakfast.

"Katie, can you pour yourself a bowl of cereal?" she called from her room. Kate, ten years old, popped into the doorway.

"Yes, Mom." She stood looking at her mother, worry creasing her face.

"I'll be okay, kiddo," Ellen said, wishing she could hold her daughter and comfort her, but knowing it might only make her sick too. "It's just the flu, honey."

Poor Kate, Ellen lay there thinking when her daughter had gone. *My little worrier.* Again, something nagged at Ellen as if she'd forgotten something vitally important. Oh well, it would come to her. She slept the rest of the day.

When another five days had come and gone with Ellen apparently no better, her husband insisted she see the family doctor.

Ellen described her flu-like symptoms to Dr. Peterson. The kindly old physician, who'd known her many years, scribbled some notes on a pad before him. He sat there looking perplexed, hands pressing into his eyes, his wire-rimmed glasses atop his bald head.

"By all standards you are the epitome of health dear girl. I can't see a single thing wrong with you. If it was the flu though, you'd have certainly shaken it by now." His glasses back in place, he tapped on the pad with his ballpoint pen. "Let's order you up some blood work, shall we? That's as good a start as any." He stood and shook Ellen's hand, giving her the script for blood work. "I'll see you back here in a few weeks, but call me if you get any worse." Dr. Peterson turned to go.

"Maybe it's just stress, Doc," Ellen offered, hand on his arm. "Hope it's nothing serious." She looked down at the floor.

"I think you'll be fine," the doctor said. "Get the blood work and we'll talk."

Ellen almost brushed off the blood test. Her stomach felt better than it had in a while. She thought better of it at the last minute though.

The phone rang on January ninth, two days later.

"May I speak with Ellen Martino?" the voice on the other end of the phone inquired.

"This is she." Ellen stood clutching the phone, waiting.

"This is Sue from Dr. Peterson's office," the voice continued. "Doctor would like to see you for an appointment."

Ellen's stomach dropped. *What on earth was this about? What did he find?*

She made an appointment for the following Tuesday as early as possible.

Ellen sat on the edge of the examination table, upset with herself for not insisting that Ray come with her. Oh well, whatever it was, she would handle it. She'd talked with God this morning and felt His calm, reassuring presence.

Dr. Peterson walked through the door and after shaking Ellen's hand, pulled a chair close to her and sat down.

"Okay, Doc, now you're scaring me."

"No, no, my dear," the doctor began. "Not to worry. All your results were fine. Uh, I have a question for you though." He looked down at the floor, a flush coloring his cheeks. "Uh, when was your last menstrual cycle?"

It hit Ellen all of a sudden. The thing she'd forgotten. She'd been so busy with the holidays this year her skipped period hadn't even been a concern to her.

"Well, I think it was in early November," Ellen said, her heart missing a beat or two.

"You're going to have a baby."

"Doc, that's not possible. I mean, I, I'm thirty nine years old. Women my age don't have babies."

"Oh," Dr. Peterson chuckled. "I can assure you, they do." He stared directly at her now. "The problem isn't your age though, my dear. The problem is your past history with carrying your pregnancies to term. You lost two babies from what I remember after Kate, right?"

"Yes I did. Oh my God, Dr. Peterson." Ellen began to cry then. "This is really true, isn't it? Oh, I feel way too old. And what if, what if I can't carry this one either?"

Dr. Peterson moved his chair closer to Ellen, practically whispering though it was only the two of them in the room. "Ellen, I've known you a very long time. I knew your mother also, and your aunts. I'm going to ask you to consider something. With the family history, it may not be a good idea to even try and carry this baby to term."

"What are you saying?" Ellen asked through her tears. She shuffled through her purse, pulling at tissues, wadding them under her nose.

"I mean look at your aunts. Both had late pregnancies, and one didn't make it out of the delivery room. Ellen, I'm afraid it's too risky for you. You practically hemorrhaged last time. Have you forgotten that?"

She hadn't. The last pregnancy, about eight years ago had been awful. One day while she was hanging clothes in the back yard, she'd felt a terrible ripping pain in her lower back. She'd left the basket of laundry, running into the house, barely made it to the phone to call Ray, then doubled over onto the floor. When her husband had come home to meet the ambulance, Ellen had already lost so much blood, she was cold and pale. She had lost the baby shortly after that.

Defiantly, Ellen looked at the doctor. "It'll be different this time, doc. I know it will. Did you know I was talking with God this morning? And did you further know I felt a peace, a reassurance that everything would be okay? I'm not worried."

"Ellen, for your own safety and health, I'm asking you

to consider an abortion."

"Never," she spat. "Never in a million years would I even think of it. This is a miracle baby, Dr. Peterson. A miracle. I admit, I'm a little older than I would've liked to be, but if God chose for me to have this little one now, then He knows what He's doing." Ellen scooted down from the table, grabbed her purse and left the room.

Later that night, in bed, Ellen told Ray the whole story. He held her closely as she sniffled into the covers.

"Oh Ray, I'm so sorry. I feel it's all my fault."

"Nonsense, honey. It certainly took two of us. I'm concerned though." He pressed his lips to her forehead. "I don't want anything to happen to you. You're my world, Ellen. I don't think I could go on without you."

They lay for a while in the dark, holding one another, Ellen crying softly into her husband's nightshirt, while he stroked her wavy hair.

The night Ellen's water broke, they had just gone to bed. Kate was already asleep when Ray shook his daughter gently awake. "Katie, wake up, honey. It's time to take your mom," was all he said.

Kate's eyes opened, and her face broke into a glorious smile. "Oh Daddy, may I please come with you and

Momma?"

"I wish I could take you, honey, but Grandma Bettina is waiting for you. I already called her. You're to stay with her a day or so. Come on, let me help you get a few things ready." Ray quickly packed an overnight bag for his daughter. Ellen was already waiting in the old Buick, her own bag packed and ready. The family made the ten minute drive to Ray's mother's house, and Grandma Bettina enfolded Katie lovingly into her arms.

Never had anything looked more beautiful. After eight hours in a relatively uneventful labor, the pink-skinned baby with the scrunchy face was the loveliest thing Ellen had ever laid eyes on. She was so happy. Her perfect little boy. . .

~*~

"So you see, Kate," Mom said, dabbing her eyes with a Kleenex I'd given her, "It wasn't as easy as you'd thought. Matthew was our miracle baby. Nobody realizes just how much of a miracle though." Mom stretched, as I poured her another glass of iced tea.

"Wow, Mom. I never realized your health was at stake. You were very brave."

"Did you know the name Matthew means 'Gift from

God?'" Mom asked. When I shook my head, she continued. "Yes, we just loved the name, but when I looked it up later in the old Bible, I saw what it meant, and realized just how true it was."

"Well he certainly felt like a gift to me," I said, getting up to clear the few dishes on the table before us. "I was so excited about having a baby brother. I'd felt lonely through the years. I never knew you'd lost other children though. Why didn't you ever tell me?"

"There was no need to worry you, Kate. I always tried to protect you."

"Mom," I began, as I picked up my own cool glass of tea. "Did you ever waver for just a moment? I mean, did you ever consider not having the baby?"

"Not for a minute, Kate. I knew I was going to have him, or die trying. But I knew God would carry us both through. I never doubted."

I stood there quietly thinking. Mom's faith amazed me. When faced with the hardest decision of her life, she calmly gave it over to God.

While I lay in bed that night, I mulled over Mom's story. What would I have done if faced with the same decision? I hoped I would be courageous as she had been.

I turned over, away from Steve, pulling the covers up to my chin, shivering in the air-conditioned room. I thought about Mom's faith, and how differently she felt than me. My parents had been attending a non-denominational church for the last few years. I had kept my comments to myself, but secretly wondered if they turned into holy rollers. I had been brought up as a strict Catholic girl, attending Catholic school, receiving all the sacraments. But my faith had been hollow, nothing more. I didn't understand the mass and all the strange rituals. I never looked beyond all that was familiar. My parents, however, had been searching, seeking, always looking for more where their faith was concerned. Would I ever find it, whatever it was?

~*~

When I awoke the morning of September 11 to the beauty of the glorious Tuesday, I felt refreshed from one of the best night's sleep in a long time. Steve and I had been making plans for a little getaway trip, and I had finalized the details last evening, content with the upcoming romantic weekend for two. It had been such a long time since we'd gone anywhere alone, and our son was going to stay with my brother. Two bachelors, a weekend of movies, popcorn, video games and pizza. All of us were looking forward to it.

Mark, my sleepyhead, had not wanted to get out of bed today. He and his dad had stayed up a little later than usual working on a project for health class. Since Steve taught at the local high school, he and Mark were on different schedules. He always left a full hour before our son, and satisfied with the heart and lungs made from clay, Steve kissed me goodbye and told me not to wait for dinner tonight, one of those mandatory meetings was in the works.

I dropped Mark off at the middle school, and then headed to my job at The Times. A little deadline was due for an article about our local library, celebrating its fiftieth year in existence. Marsha Gray, a local writer, spent hours researching facts for me, and had put together a very nice couple of paragraphs for me to insert into tomorrow's paper.

I arrived at the office around 8:15. Gathering all my paperwork, I sat at my desk, organizing the words into coherent sentences. A cup of coffee sat next to me, untouched, while I cut and pasted, then cut some more. I was just starting to like what I saw before me when Jodi

Branson, a nice lady I'd worked with for some time, rushed into my cubicle.

"Kate, did you hear what happened?" The look on her face scared me. A thousand possibilities entered my mind.

"What's up, Jodi?" I asked, forcing myself to sound more cheerful than I felt at the moment.

"A plane crashed into one of the towers of the World Trade Center."

Words that would change my life in an instant. I felt faint and sick, and the tiny bit of coffee I'd drank, and the bagel I'd eaten this morning threatened to come rushing up.

"Kate, what's the matter?" Jodi stood there as the room spun for me, faster and faster. I pushed myself away from the desk and bolted up, scattering papers across the floor.

I ran into the lobby, eyes transfixed to the television set before me. Many others were gathered around, too stunned for words, some people crying, others way too talkative for me.

Jodi came over to me then. "Kate, what is it?"

"My brother is there, Jodi. Matt flew into New York city last night for some type of meeting." My mouth felt like sandpaper. All the spit had dried up.

"He had an appointment at the World Trade Center for nine o'clock this. . ." My words trailed off as my eyes stared, transfixed at the living nightmare.

It was much worse than I'd first thought. I watched as the flames consumed the upper half of the North Tower. I watched in morbid fascination along with the others as people ran screaming on the set before me, looking back over their shoulder as the calamity unfolded.

Then the unthinkable happened. Right there before us all, another plane from out of nowhere crashed into the second tower, exploding glass and debris through the sides of the immense structure.

My legs buckled then. It was too much. Jodi put her hands under my arms and practically dragged me to a chair.

Three p.m. Steve, Mark and I arrived at my parents' house. I had tried unsuccessfully many times to call my brother's cell phone. Always the same message: All circuits are busy. Please try your call again later. If he was okay, why couldn't he find some other means to reach us? The situation felt bleak to me.

Tina was already there when we arrived, her pretty

face, blotchy with tears. She fell into my arms. "Oh Kate, oh my God. Matt called me around eight fifty this morning. He told me he felt his building shudder. He said he had just gotten to his meeting. Oh my God, Kate, what's happened?" A fresh barrage of sobs began and this time I joined her.

"Girls, come sit down in the kitchen. Let's get our heads on straight," Dad said. His face looked careworn, and his usually bright eyes appeared as if someone had let the light out of them.

Shakily, I walked arm in arm with Tina into my mother's kitchen. Mom sat at the table, her Bible open before her. She looked up as we entered, nodding to us, but resumed her silent prayers.

I let go of Tina and knelt before my mother. She reached out to me then, putting her arms around me, and the tiniest sob escaped her.

"We're not going to do this, people," Mom said, regaining composure. "There are dozens of reports of people who made it out of those buildings and are unable to contact loved ones. We sit, wait, and mostly we pray."

"I don't know if I believe in prayer right now, Mom," I said. "If God is so good, why did He let this thing happen to our country? Why is my good brother missing right now?" I looked up into her face for answers.

Tina, Steve, Dad and Mark stood silently by, waiting with me. Mom turned the pages of her worn, leather Bible and her finger rested upon something then.

"It says: *When I am afraid, I will trust in you. In God whose word I praise, in God I trust; I will not be afraid. What can mortal man do to me?*" Mom read to us. Her fingers flew through several more pages, the rustling sound of them loud in the stillness of her kitchen. "*You will not fear the terror of night, nor the arrow that flies by day, nor the pestilence that stalks in the darkness, nor the plague that destroys at midday.*"

She looked up from her readings then. I clung onto her legs while Steve pried me gently away. He held me tightly, brushing away tears that spilled from my eyes.

Mom closed her Bible. "Are any of you hungry?" She asked. "I can throw some pasta together if you want." We all shook our heads in turn, appetites forgotten for now. Dad turned the tiny television set on in the kitchen.

Clouds of debris billowed on the streets of New York City. Rescue workers picking through piles of rubble looking for survivors. Their faces all looked the same, fearful, haunted, hopeless. Again and again, the news reporters played out the events as they had unfolded this morning. Even our beloved Pennsylvania hadn't been immune. Near Somerset, a place Steve and I liked to visit often, terrorists had crashed another plane into the ground killing all aboard. So much devastation.

I left the room and headed toward my brother's old bedroom, the room Dad had taken over for his crafts. I walked through the door, picturing the way it had looked when Matt still lived here. I glanced into my own tiny bedroom, across the hall, now a guest room. I thought of all the fun my brother and I had growing up, though almost ten years separated us. We were close, he and I, and we shared many secrets, hopes and dreams in these very rooms.

The tiny pink baby, the precious gift, Matthew. The good, gentle giant, my brother. I fell to my knees in his old room then. I cried out to God from my very soul.

"Father, if you're there, I ask you for a blessing right now. I ask you for a miracle. Please, God, please take care of my brother. Let him be alright. I know I haven't spoken to you in a very long time, and I ask your forgiveness right now. I want to get to know you better. I want a relationship with your Son, like my parents have."

My eyes were closed tightly, my hands clasped before me. Images of Matt swirled around my head. Something came to me then. A tiny thought. *I will never leave you, nor forsake you.* A feeling of peace washed over me, and the feeling I wasn't alone in the room. Something like a light, feathery touch caressed my cheek. I shuddered and opened my eyes. Nothing in the room had changed, but I did. I knew then what my mother had tried telling me for years. I knew that no matter if my brother was alive or not, we'd get through this with God's help. I rose to my feet and walked from the room.

Thankfully, we were able to call off from work for the next day. Mom needed us around her, so we all settled in on couches, the guest room, wherever we could sleep. It was only nine p.m., but we were exhausted, all of us, worry had drained us and yet, the peace-filled feeling remained with me as well.

The phone had rung several times during the day, well-wishers and relatives calling to see if we'd heard anything. At about ten after nine, the phone rang again. Mom, on her way to bed, picked up the portable telephone from its base.

"Hello? Hello? I'm sorry, whoever this is, I can't

understand what you're saying." She pressed the button, disconnecting the call and placed it back. It rang again just seconds later. This time, the voice was clear.

Mom would tell us after she hung up, that nothing ever had sounded as wonderful to her as my brother's voice that night. He was staying with a bunch of others at one of the fire stations. They had set up some makeshift cots and bedding. He had waited hours for his turn to use one of the working phones since so many others were calling their own thankful loved ones.

I watched Mom's face as she spoke. We all knew it was Matt from the conversation. Mom appeared radiant, filled with peace. I looked over at my father and saw him wiping away tears that had begun to flow out of his own eyes. An almost audible sigh of relief resounded in the room. Each of us hugged one another tightly, but nobody would take the phone from Mom. This was her son, her miracle, for the second time in his life. There would be other moments to talk with him. For now, this was all we needed.

I left the others for a moment, walking back into Matt's old bedroom, again, dropping to my knees. This time, I thanked God above for His goodness. I thanked

Him for carrying my brother through and restoring him to us.

Matt arrived home two days later. Steve, Mark and I drove back to my parents' house to see him. Tina was there, and nobody could have pried her from his side. Mom had a huge Italian feast, spaghetti, meatballs, sausages and homemade rolls.

When I walked into the kitchen and saw my brother at the table, I held back tears that threatened to spill from my eyes and ran to his side. We hugged tight, tighter, tightest. I pinched him and myself to make sure we were both real.

So many questions flew around the dinner table that night. What had happened? What did it feel like? What could he tell us? But my brother wasn't quite ready to speak about it all just yet. He filled us in on some sketchy details, but said he had to sort some things out first. In time, we'd hear it all.

I walked out back with him later that night; he was just standing there, looking up at the stars in the sky. We were alone, and it felt good to have him to myself. I couldn't think of words to express my feelings.

"Kate," he began. "Glad it's you. I have to unload

some of this. I feel like I'm going crazy right now, you know what I mean?" His eyes were glassy, shiny in the darkness; the kitchen light shone out the window, illuminating his face a little.

"I keep seeing things, images, people. It all feels like a big mess to me. I don't know how or why I was so lucky, Kate. And it's bothering me. I don't know why I'm alive and so many others aren't." His voice cracked, and his shoulders began to shake with sobs.

I put my hand on his shoulder as he let forth his built-up pain. I stood there with him, silently praying that God would heal the terrible wound inside him.

"I felt the building shake, you know," he said, gaining composure. "It had to be when the first plane hit. I felt the shudder. I was in the reception room of Loeb and Horwell, the investment firm I was supposed to speak with about my agency. The secretary looked up at me from her desk, then punched a few numbers on the phone. I heard her speaking to someone, and it never occurred to me the gravity of the situation." Matt sat then on the cement stoop outside our parents' back door. I stood above him, incredulous. I had watched events all week long, and here was someone who'd had a firsthand account of what had happened. I shivered.

"I never made it into my appointment," he continued. "By then, they were talking about evacuation of both buildings. They said someone might have planted a bomb or something, and we all should begin to leave in a calm fashion.

I started walking with some others toward the elevators nearest us, when a voice came over a loudspeaker telling everyone to go back to their offices, it was all under control. So, I went back into Loeb and Horwell's pulled out my briefcase and was thumbing through my speech, when another shudder hit. This time it was much worse. Chaos started to unfold and someone screamed, 'We're under attack!' I threw my paperwork down, and started running again but they weren't letting anyone use the elevators by this time. It was mass confusion in the stair wells. People crawling over one another, and by then I heard what had happened. Someone said planes were exploding into buildings. I was on the seventy- sixth floor, Kate, just two floors down from where it hit. Do you realize what it's like living with that knowledge?"

I didn't answer. I knew he wasn't done speaking.

"A couple of flights down, I saw a woman carrying another woman, practically dragging her, you know? The woman was so bloody, she barely had a face. She looked at a bunch of us as we ran, asking for help. I passed her, I was so scared at first, but then I just couldn't go on. I walked back up the stairs and found them again. I scooped the bleeding lady into my arms, Kate, and I carried her down the rest of the stairs."

Here, he paused again, and it felt like the quiet was going to stretch out forever this time.

"I never stopped to think how tired my arms were with that lady in them. I just kept moving, knowing I had to save her, get her to safety. When I reached the bottom level, some emergency personnel were there, and they took her from me and I never saw her again. I don't know if she's alive or dead.

The lobby was a crazy mess, people milling around, shocked, some running. I saw things I can't talk about now as I left the building. I don't think I'll ever forget. . ."

"Matt, it's okay," I said. "You don't have to tell me all this." He interrupted me before I said another word.

"No, Kate, I want to. I need to." He sighed heavily and continued. "I felt so bad for some of the people on the street, bruised, battered. I just started asking if I could be of help to any of them. I was able to get some of them to ambulances, others, I'm just not sure. That's what hurts the most, not knowing.

When the towers started to crumble and we all had to run for our lives, I didn't look back after that. I couldn't. Right then, nothing seemed more important to me than self-preservation, making it out of there. I knew I'd come so far, and to not see you, Mom, Dad and Tina again, well, it wasn't an option at that point. So I ran and ran."

"Matt, are you trying to clear your conscience, is that what this is all about?" I asked. "You did the best you could. I don't know of many people who would have stopped and helped as much as you did. The way I see it, you're a hero, brother."

"No, Kate, I'm no hero. Some of the real heroes didn't survive that day. The real heroes are laying under piles of rubble, policemen, firemen."

I sat down next to my brother on the stoop. The only sound in the dark was his occasional sniffle. I wished for words to say to him. Words of comfort.

"When we got to the fire station later that night, I did as much as I could for the people around me. I didn't need a bed. I knew I wouldn't get much sleep, if any. So I worked alongside some emergency personnel, making sure people had bottled water and blankets. It was the least I could do."

I sat there incredulous. Here was my thirty year-old brother telling me the most unthinkable story, a story that was true. He had survived a disaster, one of the worst in our country. He had done heroic deeds that day, no matter how he looked at it. I could never view him in the same way again. A lump formed in my throat, and I felt proud of Matt. So very proud that he had been courageous at a time when planes driven by insane madmen thought they were doing the will of God. People like my brother were the heroes. They survived and would tell their stories for many years to come. Tonight, somewhere else in our country, someone was alive because of my brother. I could feel it. I thanked God again silently.

~*~

In spring of 2002, Matt and Tina wed in a very small ceremony. Steve and I were in the bridal party and if I do say so myself, we looked pretty darn good for a couple in their early forties. Mom looked beautiful as mother of the groom, and Dad, well, I always said he was one of the most handsome men in the world.

While we danced that night to Kool and the Gang, The Village People, and Frank Sinatra, I looked over at the wedding table. Matt and Tina sat close together, their lips touching for a brief moment, as forks clinked on glasses for them to kiss. I sighed, holding onto Steve's hand, my other arm around his shoulder, closing my eyes and feeling more blessed than I'd ever been. So many things had happened in my family through the years, but never before had I realized just how much God carried us through. As I danced with my husband, my partner for life, I whispered in his ear. "I love you so much, Steve. Dance the night away with me."

CHAPTER 5

Potter's Clay

May, 2003

"*Is* this Kate Anderson?" the voice on the phone asked while I was rushing out the door. I answered a little out of breath, and very annoyed. I was running late. Mom had an important doctor's appointment today, and she'd kill me if we didn't get there at least an hour early.

"Yes, this is she." I said, gathering my questions for the doctor which were scribbled on random pieces of paper, shoving them into a folder, and beginning the search for car keys which had decided to play hide and seek this morning.

"This is Carol Morris at the Bunker Publishing Agency. We received your manuscript *Pietro's Song* and would like to publish it in our upcoming quarterly."

I halted in mid step, my lost car keys, paperwork and even Mom forgotten for the briefest moment. "Would you say that again please?" I asked, and sat down hard into a kitchen chair, endless possibilities entering my mind.

"Yes, well, as I said. My name is Carol Morris. I read over your manuscript several times and we'd love to work with you. The knowledge and research you did on your great-grandfather is impeccable and I believe his story will reach out and touch so many others who are interested in ancestry and genealogy."

Well, I'll be... "Oh Miss Morris, that's wonderful, thank you," I said, remembering my manners finally. "I'd be thrilled to talk this over with you at greater length." I saw my car keys sticking out of my purse just then. *Just where I've always kept them.*

"Shall we meet next week sometime?" she asked me. "Let's say, over lunch on Wednesday, perhaps?"

I gulped and found myself saying yes. My stomach twisted and knotted. This is what I'd been waiting for; a chance to break into print, finally. After all the years of working at our local newspaper, and all the editing I'd done. Someone was recognizing me and my own skills as a writer.

I hung the phone up, so many thoughts swirling through my head. A published piece! I couldn't wait to share my news with Steve and my family. On the tail of that thought, however, self-doubt threatened with ill timing. What if I failed somehow? What if once the article was published, people really didn't like it, really didn't see what I was trying to convey from my heart? Worse still, what if I didn't truly have talent and this was just some 'filler' article to take up space? Insecurity, my old pal, my lifelong bosom buddy settled in my brain and made itself comfortable.

~*~

The lights on the stage shone down hot and bright. The cast members of the play from my senior year delivered their lines with precision. Not me, though. I was due on stage in a few moments and I forgot my own lines. Quickly, I tried rushing around trying to find a script somewhere. Frantic, I tore through the music room, scattering sheets of music, unable to find one. I ran down the hallway of my old high school, trying to remember which locker was mine. Think, Kate, think. My script was in there, I just knew it. I reached the locker and almost screamed. The combination lock hung there, a clunky sentinel barring me from reaching my goal. The numbers. I didn't remember the combination numbers. . .

I rolled over in bed and threw the covers off, trying to shake the remnants of the old recurring dream, my upper body drenched in perspiration for the third night in a row. I had to get up and change my stupid nightshirt once again. I lay back down, waving the sheet above my body like a giant fan when I woke poor Steve up.

"Kate, what is it? You having a bad dream, honey?" He moved over toward me, trying to pull me closer to him. I resisted, keeping him at arm's length. He would only make me sweat more.

"Kind- of," I answered. What was I going to say? *Steve, I believe I've been having night sweats. And oh, by the way, I had the stupid dream again. You know, the one where I can't do anything right?*

"How's your mom taking her news from her appointment this morning?" Steve asked, rolling onto his back.

"You know Mom. Stoic and faith-filled to the end. She practically told the doctor off when he mentioned she had the beginning of dementia." I whispered, not wanting to wake our son Mark. "She said his tests were stupid and they didn't know what they were looking for anyway."

Steve laughed. "Your mom is an Italian tank. She's an amazing woman."

We lay there, the tiffany style nightlight casting a cozy glow into our room. My few moments of heat passed and I turned toward my husband, laying my hand across his chest.

"Steve, I was going to wait until tomorrow at dinner to tell you my other news."

He turned toward me then with a start. "What is it, Kate?" I could hear the concern in his voice.

"A magazine publishing company called this morning. They want to publish my manuscript."

Steve bolted up. "Honey, that's wonderful! Wow, I'm so proud of you." He gathered me into his arms and I couldn't share his enthusiasm. "Kate? What's the matter?" Apparently he was very good at reading my body language and silence after twelve years of marriage.

"Oh, Steve, I don't know. Just so much is going on in my head. Yes, this is what I wanted more than anything. But I'm not sure people will really like it, or accept it. I'm not sure I'm good enough."

Steve kissed my forehead then my neck. He held me

tightly in our dimly lit bedroom. Almost rocking me like a small child. My armor, my strength. He never gave up on me even when negativity threatened and old ghosts rose up to haunt me with their taunting. Bits and pieces of that stupid dream unsettled me. The funny thing, I understood its meaning with perfect clarity. It was a performance dream and I always had it when I didn't feel good enough for something.

"Kate, you'll be fine, and people will love your writing." His breath tickled my face as he whispered in the dimness. "I wish you could see yourself the way I see you. The way your family and people that meet you for the first time see you."

He ran his hands over my body, and I melted into him, forgetting all about this crazy day, Mom's news, and the phone call from the magazine publisher.

Sunday morning, my brother phoned before we headed out to church. "Hey sis, what're you up to?" Matt's pleasant voice always made me smile.

"Just getting the troops ready for church, Matt," I answered. I fidgeted with my purse, trying to rearrange some of the contents. "How's married life?"

"It's great," he said. "Tina's amazing. I'm worried

about Mom, though. Don't you think she should be on some type of medication?"

"Matt, if you were there with us Friday, you wouldn't feel this way. Mom's fine. I mean it, really fine. They said she has the start of a mild form of dementia, and they aren't extremely concerned with it right now." I fished old packages of gum and cough drops out of my purse, rummaging through for other items to discard.

"Kate, it's just that I don't want to see her go downhill fast like Gram did. You remember the stories Mom told us of how her mother forgot where she lived?"

"Matt, we'll keep a close eye on her. Try not to worry. It won't happen overnight. And when it's time to get her on some type of medication, we will." I paused for a moment. "And try praying about it." I added, feeling smug for throwing in a hint.

He chuckled then and said he would do just that. We hung up and I gave silent thanks for my amazing brother. The big guy with a big heart.

After church, Steve wanted to take a drive. We left Monroeville, headed west toward Ohio. I wasn't sure what he was up to and he had that look as if he was hiding something. Mark piped up from the back seat several times, "Where are we going Dad?" But Steve just shook his head and smiled that adorable crooked smile of his.

We entered the quaint town of Hanover an hour and a half later and parked in front of an old building in their downtown district. It resembled a courthouse, huge pillars, and large granite staircase. The name on the front puzzled me, though. It read: Baltimore Hudson.

"Okay, I give up, wise guy," I said. "What on earth is this place?"

"You'll see." Steve motioned for me to wait while he opened his car door, walking around to my side, and with a slight bow, opened the door for me. He extended his hand like a limo driver and pulled me out of the car. Mark chuckled in the back seat, probably thinking his dad had clearly lost his mind. Steve opened his door too, and soon the three of us were headed into the immense building.

We walked into the foyer of what appeared to be some sort of museum from the look of it. Large, marble statues adorned the corridors, expensive-looking tapestries and huge paintings hung on walls, and rooms were clearly marked with signs for different types of exhibits.

"Three please," Steve said to the slender young girl

sitting behind an ornate counter. She took the money he offered and gave three tickets to him. I walked over to a bronze plaque on the wall explaining the old building. It had housed an opera back in the 1930's, a courthouse in the 50's and now a museum. Two wealthy businessmen, Frank Baltimore and Ronald Hudson owned it back in the day and donated it to the community to continue to be a place where arts and creativity blossomed.

"Come on," Steve urged, almost pulling me along as Mark tried to keep up with his father's pace.

The first room we entered showed me the reason we were there. It had a placard which read: *Titanic Exhibit*. I squealed and clapped my hands. Mark's eyes were enormous. This was the travelling exhibit I'd heard about which housed many of the artifacts found on the ocean floor from the ill-fated ship. The *Titanic* fascinated my son and me. We spent hours researching facts, watching anything The Discovery Channel played about it, and of course we loved the fictional movie version.

"Steve, I can't believe this. How did you hear of it?" I looked over at him, and he was watching me with that adorable smile, enjoying, almost soaking in my reactions.

"Are you happy, Kate?" he asked.

"Words can't describe how I feel," I said and entered the dream world. We were given name tags and a little sheet with information as we walked into the first area. Each tag carried the name of a specific passenger who had sailed aboard *Titanic*. It was almost as if you were there with them, not just a spectator in a museum. I was given the name John Jacob Aster. Mark got Molly Brown, and Steve got Captain Edward Smith. We took a few minutes reading about our namesake, and then entered the heart of the museum display.

The first room housed artifacts taken from the ocean floor. Broken pieces of china, bent silverware, someone's reading glasses, a child's doll, and waterlogged books. One by one, I viewed each item, my son at my side, remarking on all of them. A lump formed in my throat as I thought about the real people who'd owned these things, the living, breathing people who used them in their short time aboard the ship. People with families and loved ones and their whole lives ahead of them.

We walked through an ornate doorway which meant to look like the doors to the grand ballroom. It was in this room my breath caught in my chest. A huge piece of the ship's hull stood before me, roped off, but near enough to touch. My hand followed the smooth planes of the structure, as Mark's did the same. It was all I could do to keep from crying.

"Kate, I'm so glad you liked it," Steve said to me as we left the final room an hour and a half later. He guided Mark and me toward another part of the building where sumptuous smells emanated from within.

"What's this?" I asked, suddenly glad I hadn't changed the dress I'd worn to church. A lavish restaurant was nestled into the wing of the museum. Maître D's in tux's stood at the door, pretty young girls in old-fashioned uniforms greeted us.

"Oh my gosh," I remarked as I realized this final leg of today's journey. The room before us looked like the formal dining area of the *Titanic*. People dressed in finery milled about and classical music from a different era played softly in the background. "Steve," I beamed. "This is the most wonderful day of my life." Mark's mouth stood open in a giant 'O'. I had to nudge him to get him moving into the room.

While we were seated at our table, Steve cleared his throat and I knew he was about to say something important. "Kate, I wanted this day to be as special for you and Mark as you both are to me. Sometimes as a family, we don't get to spend as much quality time together as I'd like." He picked up a warm roll and slathered butter atop it. A young waiter filled two crystal goblets with red wine and a Shirley Temple for our son.

"I wanted to convey to you how very proud I am of you for your accomplishments as a mother, but also as a writer." He saw I was about to protest but continued. "You don't give yourself enough credit, honey. I mean it. You're going to do great things, I can feel it."

I brushed at a tear that slid from the corner of one eye, raising my glass to Steve's as we toasted to a wonderful day together. My stomach knotted, however, thinking about meeting with the lady who'd phoned about publishing my article. I knew what Steve was trying to do. He always built me up even when I was faced with the worst case scenarios and lowest self-esteem of my life. He knew things about me nobody else did. He heard the countless stories of my childhood and teenage years, the ugly duckling time in my life where I couldn't do anything right, when young boys tormented me about my twisted body as scoliosis ravaged my spine. . .

~*~

Kate Martino, twelve years old, brushed her long straight hair as the static crackled through it. She'd put on her bell bottom jeans and pretty new top with the flowing sleeves she'd gotten for Christmas a few weeks ago. She stood in front of the full length mirror on the back of her bedroom door. She bent to her left, then her other side. Something didn't seem right. The shirt looked weird the way it hung on her skinny frame. She tried standing as straight as she could, but now her pants looked funny. The terrible words some of the boys said to her recently while they made fun of her came back with perfect clarity this morning. First Tom Parker began saying dumb things to her in English class under his breath. Then his idiotic gang of friends had joined in, all the while chanting her name, making fun of the way she walked.

Mom always tried telling her she was beautiful, she was unique. But the boys knew better. She was weird and ugly, clumsy and stupid. She couldn't even walk correctly. Kate pulled her top off and stared into the mirror. Her right side protruded in a strange way. Perhaps this was normal, the way a young girl's body was supposed to look as the teenage changes began to occur. She stared for a while and then called for her mother.

Kate's mom poked her head through the door of Kate's room wrestling with two year old Matthew, trying to get him dressed. Kate's baby brother wriggled in her arms when their mother decided to give up. "What's up, Katie?"

All of a sudden, Kate became extremely self-conscious. She put her hands across her body, hugging her arms to herself. "Mom, do you see something weird with me?" She'd never told her mother a thing about the boys and their teasing. Knowing Mom, she'd be at the school in no time, telling them off, embarrassing her further.

"You look like you're slouching," her mother said. Just then little Matt ran into the room, free and unclothed, his favorite toy monster clutched in his hands.

"Mom, get him out of here," Kate sighed. "I can't have any privacy." Ellen shooed her son from the room, promising him homemade chocolate chip cookies if he was a good boy.

When she turned back to her daughter, Kate noticed a puzzled look on her face. "Kate, it's odd. Can't you stand straight?"

Kate felt her lip tremble. "No, Mom, that's just it. I've

been noticing for a month or so now, something's weird about my clothes. At least I thought it was my clothes."

"Take your hands away from your chest," Ellen said. "Trust me, I know what you look like."

Shyly, Kate removed her hands from in front of her body. Her mom gasped. "Oh, Kate, something's not right." At those words, Kate did start to cry. Ellen put an arm around her daughter, stroking her back. Kate would find out much later that her mother had felt her shoulder blade protruding strangely from her back as she held her that day.

"Let's call Dr. Thomas," Ellen said. "It's probably nothing, maybe just a growth spurt or something. Get dressed for school, Kate."

On a Friday afternoon in early March, the Martino family drove to downtown Pittsburgh to a specialist clinic for children. In the month since Kate showed Mom her deformity, the teasing at school worsened considerably. Now the popular girls started snickering when Tom and his minions began their nasty chanting. Sometimes between classes, Kate would run into the girl's restroom, locking herself into a stall. With tears streaming down her face, she'd ask God why she had to endure this. She awoke each morning sick to her stomach, trying to think of ways to miss school, anything to not have to confront her horrible tormentors. Day after day however, she made it through, trying to ignore the taunting remarks, all the while hating herself.

Doctor William Stone sat behind a desk, x- rays of Kate's spine on the wall next to him. Kate, Ellen, and Ray stared speechless at what the image showed. The spine in Kate's back curved into a crazy 'S' shape.

"Your daughter has scoliosis," the doctor said in a matter of fact voice. The bottom of Kate's stomach dropped. She knew it. She was a freak. The boys were right. Whatever this was, it wasn't something normal. She hung her head.

"Doctor," Ray said. "Can you give it to us in layman's terms please? We want to know what's going on with our little girl." Ray laid a hand on his daughter's knee as he sat next to her. Ellen linked her own arm through his.

"Scoliosis is curvature of the spine," the doctor explained. "We're unsure of why certain young people get this, but it could be one of you had something similar when you were young." He tapped a ballpoint pen against the desk as he spoke. "You all don't have to look so glum. There is corrective surgery for this. We do it all the time. It's not without risks, however, but the prognosis should be pretty good." He stopped speaking and the only sound in the room was the sniffling of Kate and Ellen as their tears began to flow.

Kate went through a series of pre-tests, blood work, more x- rays and was scheduled for surgery in early June of 1972. She met other girls during some of her appointments who'd already gone through the procedure. They looked wonderful. Could it be possible? Would she, too, be normal once again? Would she fit in and feel like all the other girls in her school, girls who hadn't had to worry about boys making fun of them? Girls who didn't have to worry about much else except which boy liked them.

The day she walked through the massive doors of Children's Hospital in Pittsburgh, Kate's hands trembled as she clutched onto her mother's arm. Her stomach felt like a twisted knot of fear. Uncertainty lay before her. She would be in this place for three full weeks. She would undergo a nine hour major surgery with the stark possibility of paralysis if the surgery didn't go well. The upper part of her body would be encompassed by an enormous plaster cast. Her legs felt weak beneath her.

After check-in, Kate was ushered to a ward with other young girls on the fifth floor of the hospital. Nothing would prepare Kate for the sights she witnessed in the room. Girls lay in hospital beds, some with tubes running from their arms to a device connected behind them. Some had metal pieces encircling their heads, and others, huge plaster casts covering their upper torso. Machines beeped, nurses with careworn faces brought medication, extra pillows and kind words to these children. Kate wanted to run from this room of sickness. Run and never look back. She looked at Mom and Dad with a heavy heart.

"Okay, kiddo, let's get you to your bed," Mom said, carrying Kate's bags with her. Dad had a sick expression on his face, but when he caught his daughter looking, he broke into a beaming smile. Kate put her simple belongings into a little stand next to the empty bed which would be her home for a time. A pale girl, a little older, with dark curly hair, came over to her.

"Hi, I'm Martha. I've been here many times for spinal surgery. This is my last one. They said I'll be able to walk normal soon." She stuck her frail hand out to shake

Kate's hand. Her thin shoulders slumped and her small body twisted unnaturally yet she had the sweetest smile that put Kate at ease instantly.

"I'm in the bed next to you. If you need anything, just give a holler." Martha limped off to help another little girl who was struggling with a coloring book and crayons in her bed.

Once Ellen and Ray left for the evening with promises to return early the next day, Kate lay silently in the hospital bed. She sniffled into the covers, trying to be as quiet as possible. Fear lay on her like a huge blanket she couldn't shake. Loneliness suffocated her as she thought about her parents and brother. Panic tickled at her, thoughts bombarding her of living out the rest of her life in a wheelchair. Her bedmate Martha came over to her.

"Don't cry, Katie. It'll be okay. You're lucky you aren't all ugly and deformed like me. You'll be beautiful when it's over." Martha stroked Kate's hair with her hand. Kate stopped sniffling and managed a smile.

Her hair was cut short for the procedure, since the body cast would rest against the back of her head. Ellen and Ray arrived as early as possible on the morning of the surgery, holding Kate's hands as they prayed with her.

Nurses and other children quieted for this special time. A young anesthesiologist walked into the room and cleared his throat.

"We're all ready for you, Kate," he said, beaming a huge, friendly smile at her. "Mr. and Mrs. Martino, she's in good hands. I'll watch out for her." He began to wheel Kate's bed into the hallway.

Ellen and Ray walked alongside Kate as she was rolled down the hall and into an elevator. Already groggy from an injection she'd been given earlier to calm her, Kate managed a weak smile to her parents. The lights on the ceiling blurred as she was carted into the operating room.

Gentle hands lifted Kate from her bed to be placed onto the operating table. Huge, bright lights shone overhead and at least a dozen masked faces peered at her. Everyone was very kind and wished her well, as she counted backward from one hundred when an intravenous solution was placed into her arm. Her last thought: *Please God; I don't want to be paralyzed.*

Kate awoke to a soft voice and the feeling of someone shaking her shoulder. "Kate, Kate, wake up. Would you wiggle your toes please?" As bleary as Kate felt, she obliged and the toes wiggled, causing the nurse whose face came into focus to smile. A 'thumbs up' sign to Kate told her that she was going to be fine. Her body was encompassed by a huge plaster cast, and Kate slid her hands down the sides of it, the rough texture of it a lumpy terrain.

When Ellen and Ray joined their daughter in the recovery room, Kate smiled sleepily at them, barely able to keep her eyes open.

The next few days, Kate was placed into a private room. Strange patterns and colors appeared on the ceiling before her as the morphine took effect. She was vaguely aware of several intravenous tubes taped onto her hands and arms, a tube inserted into her nose which led into her stomach. When a few days had gone by and the equipment taken from her body, Kate was encouraged to sit up. Although searing pain shot through her back at first, nothing felt more freeing than beginning to walk again supported by a nurse on either side.

Before she left the hospital, Kate walked into her friend Martha's new private room. The young girl had the same type of tubes protruding from her body, but her color looked all wrong. Her skin had a bluish cast to it, and her breathing was irregular. Martha's mother sat off to the side, stroking her daughter's hand.

"Is she going to be okay?" Kate asked. Her eyes went back to Martha's face.

"No, honey," Martha's mother said, "She's not." Her eyes looked glassy and puffy as if she'd been crying for a very long time. A man walked into the room then, her husband perhaps, and put a hand on the woman's shoulder.

"Our baby is going to be with the Lord soon. I guess God has other plans for her. She may not make it through the night." The smallest sob escaped the woman then.

Kate walked over to Martha, disbelief and overwhelming sadness heavy upon her. Tears fell from her eyes, clouding her vision of the girl who'd been so kind. "I want to thank you, Martha, for being there for me. You were brave when I wasn't. I'll never forget you." She patted the girl's arm, and then left the room with a silent prayer to God for her friend.

Kate's comeback was long and grueling. The plaster cast which encased her upper body to just below her hips was uncomfortable and cumbersome. Her head was tilted into the air as the neck part of the cast rested just below her chin and followed all the way around the back of her head. It took time, but Kate learned to walk, sit, but mostly lay flat in bed with a book propped open above her in her hands.

The teacher that came in the fall to tutor her was a nice older lady who spent more time gabbing with Ellen than teaching Kate. By the time December rolled around, Kate was able to go back to school in a much smaller cast, hidden under the smock tops that were in style.

Tom Parker and his notorious gang treated Kate more kindly when she returned. Some of the girls who'd never talked with her before began to want to know her better. By the following school year, Kate even had been asked to her first Christmas dance. . .

~*~

As our family finished the grand meal before us in the elegant restaurant, I sat back thinking about how far I'd come, yet how far I still had to go. There were other times in my life when my self-esteem would suffer. We left that day, the three of us with laughter and so much talk of all that we'd seen and learned in that lovely museum. I'd completely forgotten my upcoming appointment for now.

I called my mother Tuesday evening. "Hey, Mom, how's everything?"

"Well, your father is driving me crazy," she said. "He wants to take his dollhouses and miniatures to a craft fair. I told him he's nuts. Nobody wants all that junk."

I chuckled to myself. The best way to approach this was to be proactive. "Mom, maybe it's not such a bad idea. Why don't you bake something wonderful and go along with him? This way you could make a little money for yourself. And nobody and I mean nobody can bake like you."

I heard the change in her voice then. "Hmmm, maybe that's not such a bad idea," she said. "What do you think I should make?"

"Well, why don't you start with your Pineapple Upside Down cake, maybe some of those Chocolate Chip Oatmeal cookies, and maybe the low fat Brownie recipe for people who may be watching their weight. I think you'll do well, Mom. I can come over and help you. When is the fair?"

"It's in a month, the week before Father's Day."

"Okay, I can come over this weekend. We'll begin then." I switched the subject. "Mom, I don't know if you remember, but I have that appointment tomorrow at lunch with the lady from the magazine publishing company."

"You think I forgot that?" Mom crabbed on the other end. "I may be starting to forget some things, Kate, but come on, give me a little credit." She laughed then, and it was good for me to hear it.

"I'm scared, Mom. I never had an opportunity like this before."

"Kate, you never have given yourself enough credit for anything. You have talent. You're my daughter for goodness sakes."

I smiled to myself. Yes, Kate Anderson daughter of Ellen Martino. I could do this. I could do anything.

"Give 'em heck," she said. "Don't let them see you sweat. Then call me later when you hear the good news, okay?"

"Yes, Mom, I will. Thank you. Love you." I hung up.

The next afternoon I sat in the booth at LaVita, a little Italian restaurant near my office. Carol Morris was due in just a few minutes. My breath came in shallow gasps, my palms began to sweat, and I felt dizzy. I realized I was in the throes of an all-out panic attack.

Breathe deeply through the nose and a long exhale through the mouth. I remembered my mantra with practiced expertise. Just as I stopped hyperventilating, an attractive, older woman walked over to me, her arms filled with binders.

"Are you Kate?"

I shook my head yes, and got up to shake hands with the woman as she laid her things upon the end of the table.

"I'm Carol Morris. Nice to meet you." She sat and smoothed her hands over her gray suit. "So, what's the lunch specialty?"

"They have an eggplant parm sandwich to die for," I answered, eyeing the stack of notebooks and paperwork.

"Is it too early for a drink?" she asked, signaling the waiter. "I'll have a glass of Chardonnay," she said. "A glass of ice water with lemon also. How about you, Kate?"

I shook my head. "Diet Coke for me, please."

"I wanted to tell you a little about our company," Carol began. She pulled papers from one of the binders and laid them before me. "It began over twenty years ago and quickly became one of the most prestigious reads next to the larger name periodicals. Then when the internet took off, we started publishing online as well. We are read by over a million households. Articles such as yours are of particular interest to us since genealogy is something people can relate to. Everyone wants to know about grandma, grandpa, etcetera."

Our waiter returned with Carol's glass of wine. I secretly wished to snatch it up and drain it in a few gulps, but sipped my diet drink delicately, continuing to listen as she droned on about her wonderful company.

Our orders placed, Carol got down to the reason for her visit. "Kate, we really like your writing style. You have a way of conveying things from the heart. I felt like I was right there with you as you researched facts about your great-grandfather. I felt like I was on the boat with him, making the journey to the new world. Your style is simple, but powerful."

My head spun again, but in a good way this time. She really did like my writing. "Thank you, Carol," I said, leaning a little closer to view other papers she slid toward me.

"These are some simple contracts to sign if you would, giving us the rights to this printed piece. You won't be able to submit it to anyone else for a period of at least two years."

Our food arrived then, and Carol scooped up the papers, pushing them aside as she dug into the huge sandwich oozing sauce from its sides. I watched her enjoying the eggplant, all the while still trying to talk through mouthfuls of food.

I had to get back to the office, so after boxing the rest of my uneaten food, I signed my life away on several lines without a second thought. *God, I hope I just did the right thing.*

"It was so good to meet you," I said, getting up and placing the Styrofoam container under my arm. "Thank you so much for this opportunity." I shook Carol's hand once more and we parted with promises of speaking again sometime next week by telephone.

While I was walking out the door of the restaurant, trying to juggle my container of food, purse and car keys, I absently bumped into someone strolling in. Looking up, I almost cried out. It was Antonio, my first husband. Though he had dark sunglasses on his still handsome face, I knew it was him. He laughed heartily with the young woman who accompanied him, oblivious of me. My stomach churned, heart racing, while a feeling of utter dread stole over me.

When the weekend rolled around, Mom and I bustled around her kitchen, tube pan, cookie sheets, measuring cups and spoons banging. I sipped a cup of piping hot decaf coffee, the steam rising and the liquid burning my lips a bit.

"What's with the decaf today?" Mom asked. She had her salt and pepper hair tied up in a scarf this morning. The ends stuck up wildly and her glasses slid down her nose giving her a comical look.

"I've been a bit shaky lately, that's why," I answered, reaching under the cupboard for the flour and baking powder.

Mom chuckled then. "Hmm, let's see. You're forty-two now, Kate. Could it be you are doing the menopause thing?"

I turned to her almost with a snarl. "What do you mean?"

"Listen, kid, I went through the change early. It's a trait in my family. My aunt was already done at thirty nine. Mom was done by forty five. It's no big deal."

I stopped what I was doing and looked at Mom. "I've been having night sweats. And I've been having stupid panic attacks again. Do you think it's all related?"

Mom walked over to me, putting a hand on my arm. "Kate, yes I do. You know I had 'nervous issues' when I was your age. Your father was afraid I was losing my mind. It's all part of the game of life."

All part of the game. I hated it. I wanted to be young again. Not this partially dried up version of who I once was. My insecurities had threatened recently and brought back a barrage of memories from my teenage years and with them, the imminent approach of mid-life. It felt unfair. I had been a late bloomer, and it felt as if time was ticking by way too fast. Steve and I met in our late twenties. I got pregnant with Mark a year later. My young life had been snatched from me by. . . I couldn't bear the thought. It had been a long time since I'd said his name out loud. A very long time since Mom and I spoke of the man who'd almost ruined my life. Seeing him this past week had almost put me over the edge. I'd never tell Mom he was back in town.

"Mom, do you ever see Mrs. Stinelli?" Mom turned toward me, a look on her face that was unreadable. I could swear I saw her pale a little.

"Why did you bring that crazy lady up, Kate?" Mom

banged her metal mixing bowl down on the table.

"I don't know. Lots of thoughts lately. I was thinking about my surgery the other day too. I put you guys through the ringer, didn't I?"

"No, honey," Mom softened. "It wasn't your fault." She picked up her wooden spoon and beat at the batter a little harder than usual. "You couldn't help what happened with your body. Curvature of the spine wasn't something you chose." She sighed, putting down the spoon looking me directly in the eyes. "Antonio, well, I can't say I blame you there either. What a charmer. None of us could have guessed what he was really like. He had us all hoodwinked."

Antonio Stinelli. A young man who'd changed the course of my early life. I wondered if he'd changed. . .

~*~

"Hey, Kate, it's Sue. Heartbeat's opening tonight. That famous Pittsburgh DJ, Fat Eddy is supposed to be there for the ribbon cutting. Please tell me we're going." Sue Collins, Kate's best friend from high school, pestered Kate on a chilly autumn afternoon. Heartbeat, the famous under twenty-one disco, would open its doors to crowds and crowds of young people. It was the first of its kind in their area.

Kate tucked the phone under her chin. She had a ton of homework due on Monday for her business English class. Bradford Business School had teachers that were thorough, but a little too strict. If Kate didn't pass the upcoming test in that stupid class, she might have to forfeit graduating her eighteen month course in high honors. She erased her answer for the fifth time in the book opened before her.

"Sue, I can't. I'm a little behind since I missed two days last week with that stupid flu. I just gotta catch up or Miss Hitchins is gonna kill me."

"Party pooper. You can work on it all day tomorrow. Come on, Kate. We haven't done anything fun for the longest time. I got my dad's car for tonight too. Please?"

Sue wore on Kate's last nerve. "Okay," Kate said, more to shut her up than anything. "I'll be ready around seven. Don't call me again today though, okay?"

Sue pulled into Kate's driveway at six-thirty that evening. Kate's dad whistled when she walked through the door.

"This isn't Sue Collins, my daughter's best friend is it? This looks more like Cinderella on her way to the ball,"

Ray said, twirling Sue around like a dancer.

"Oh stop, Dad," Kate Martino, twenty years old said, as she walked into the living room in a black silk dress, spaghetti strap shoulders, and lacy black shawl draped over them. Ray whistled again. "Ellen, I don't think we better let these two out of our site tonight."

"That's enough" Kate said, rummaging through the living room closet for her mother's small, black clutch, the one she used for weddings and special occasions.

"We're disco queens, Mr. Martino," Sue said, trying to keep a straight face.

"Well whatever you girls are, they didn't make em' like you in my day," Ray said, chuckling.

"Be careful, girls," Ellen called out from the kitchen. "No sneaking any booze in, you hear me?"

"Mother, please," Kate said as she pecked her father on the cheek. "We aren't like that."

The half hour drive to Heartbeat felt like an eternity to Kate. The high heel shoes she wore already hurt her feet, the pointy toes pinching her uncomfortably. Kate was much more used to jeans and a t-shirt. The shawl barely covered the slinky dress, and she felt chilled on the autumn night.

"You look ravishing, my dear," Sue said to her as they exited the car to wait in the long line which formed outside the huge building on the corner of the shopping mall. Loud music pulsated from within. Girls with polyester body suits and handkerchief dresses stood chewing gum, their hair teased high; compacts open before them checking their lipstick last minute. Boys in gaudy leisure suits stood with their arms crossed, some of their faces bored, others, hopeful.

When the line started moving twenty minutes later, Sue squeezed Kate's arm. "Oooh, I'm so excited. Listen, there's that new song."

The girls walked past the coat check area of the building, and headed for the main room. A glowing disco ball and roving rainbow lights lit up the floor. Bodies swayed and pulsated to the rhythm. Kate's eyes played over the people dancing, and others who stood watching. DJ Fat Eddy snapped his fingers and shuffled to the beat in one corner of the huge room. The place was packed.

"Look, Kate, there's a table over there." The girls laid their purses down and Kate barely had a chance to take a breath when Sue pulled her friend toward the dance floor. "Come on, Kate, that's my favorite song." The first notes to the Bee Gees 'Night Fever' started playing. As Kate's eyes surveyed the huge crowd, she noticed a handsome young man watching her from the edge of the dance floor. He smiled, giving her goose bumps. The girls danced to several more songs when a slow tune began playing. Kate was about to exit the floor, when the young fellow stopped her.

"Dance with me?" he asked. Kate found herself looking into the deep brown eyes of a very attractive young man, dark complexion longer brown hair, and the physique of a body builder. She looked over at Sue who gave her a 'what's the matter with you', type of look and said, "Okay."

"I've been watching you," he whispered in Kate's ear as the song played. "You're a very good dancer." He held her closely, but not uncomfortably so. *He* certainly knew how to dance, and Kate felt like a queen. "I'm Antonio. What's your name, beautiful?"

Kate felt herself turning crimson. He stared directly into her eyes. Her breath caught in her throat. "I'm Kate," she managed to say without stammering.

"Well, hello Kate," he said. "I just moved here from New Jersey with my family. I like the Pittsburgh area. You from here?"

"Yes, I'm from a small town a little north, Ambridge." The song was over and another slow tune began. Kate turned as if to leave, when Antonio gently pulled her to him again. "May I have another dance?"

When the set of slow songs was over, Antonio asked if he could join the two girls. As he sat with them, he concentrated on Kate. "Tell me all about you," he said, sliding his chair as close as possible to her. He listened attentively and then shared his own stories. The night was amazing. Kate didn't mean to ignore her friend, but Sue finally had enough.

"Kate, I'm ready to leave now." She glared at Antonio.

"I can take Kate home," Antonio said. "I'd love to as a matter of fact."

"No, but thank you, though," Kate said. The spell was broken. She wouldn't go home with someone she just met.

"May I have your phone number then?" Antonio asked. He patted his jacket pockets and came up with a scrap of paper. "I have no pen." Sue sighed and pulled one from her purse. Antonio walked the girls to their car and leaned lightly toward Kate as he opened the door for her. His lips brushed her cheek gently. "Bella. . ." he whispered.

On the drive home, Kate sat in stunned silence, spellbound. No boys in high school had ever given her that much attention, or spoken to her in that dreamy tone. *Antonio*. Even his name sounded romantic.

Sue was sullen for most of the drive. Well, it wasn't like she didn't have a good time, Kate thought. She'd danced with a few of the local boys. Sue stopped the car and put it in park in Kate's driveway. She turned toward her friend. "Listen, I'm being ridiculous. I guess I never had anyone pay that kind of attention to me before. I thought it was going to be me and you tonight. I had no idea that guy would stay with you the whole night."

Kate sat there not knowing what to say. *Her best friend. She should be happy for her.* "It's okay," she said. "I probably won't ever hear from him again anyway. Thanks, Sue. Talk to you sometime next week."

Kate would eat her words. When she'd thought she wouldn't hear from Antonio, she'd been wrong. He phoned the next day and the next night and every day after. Kate couldn't believe how wonderful he was. Flowers came to the door for her from the local florist with a card written in Italian from him. He couldn't wait to see her again.

"Wow," Ellen said one day as another small bouquet of flowers arrived for her daughter. "Looks serious. When are we going to meet this guy?"

The family decided on a Sunday evening in late October. Ellen would make one of her best Italian feasts. Then they could see for themselves if this young man was worthy of their daughter.

Sunday night, at six p.m., a knock sounded at the door. Ray answered and before him stood a very handsome young man in shirt, tie, and dress slacks. His longer hair was neatly combed and in one hand was a huge box of chocolates. Ray shook his free hand, remarking on the firm grip. Antonio had arrived. He presented Ellen with the expensive candy and a small kiss on the cheek. Kate and her brother stood off to the side. Antonio saw her and remarked on how lovely she looked. Afterward, when the family gathered in the dining room, he surprised everyone by pulling out the chair for Kate to sit.

Antonio had a way of putting everyone at ease. His impeccable manners and dry sense of humor made for a lovely evening.

Kate walked Antonio to his car a little later. He leaned to kiss her tenderly. "I don't think I've met anyone like you and your family, Cara," he said. "I must have done something good for God to bless me with all of you." Kate melted. As they said their goodbyes, Antonio promised to return in a few days.

Kate and Antonio spent all their free time with one another. The whirlwind romance blossomed quickly and soon it was Christmas. Antonio had a special evening planned for them, and a tiny package wrapped in gold foil he presented to her over dinner.

"I know it's short notice. But I've never been so certain of anything. Kate, I love you. I want to spend my life with you." He pushed the present toward her.

A thin silver ring adorned with three diamonds lay inside. Kate looked up at him. Her heart fluttered in her chest.

"Kate Martino, will you marry me?" His eyes. . . those brown eyes Kate could lose herself in for hours. She found herself saying yes.

Antonio slid his chair closer to Kate. "I'd like to get married as soon as possible. Let's try for summertime, okay?"

Kate sat there, lost in deep emotions. She stretched her slender arm, admiring the beautiful ring and the way the diamonds sparkled just so. Yet it all felt a bit surreal. The way he was pushing to get married so quickly. "Are you sure?"

"I've never been more sure of anything." Antonio put his large hand atop Kate's petite one, never taking his eyes from her face. "Kate, my parents want to take care of the whole thing."

Kate gasped. "What on earth?"

"Yes, well there's something I need to tell you." Antonio shifted uncomfortably. "My father owns a steel mill and my parents are very well off. They told me when I was younger they wanted to do this for me." Antonio blushed.

Kate sat there, stunned. She hadn't known a thing about his financial situation. How lucky could she be? Someone to pay for the whole wedding and this amazing man before her who would cherish her always. The few moments of disquiet quickly vanished.

The day of the wedding was elegance and charm. Twenty-one year old Kate looked stunning as she walked down the aisle of St. Patrick's Cathedral on the arm of her father. A huge reception followed at Ella's one of the most sophisticated establishments in the Pittsburgh area.

The young lovebirds honeymooned in the Bahamas, paid for by the Stinelli family. Kate couldn't help but feel as if she'd soon wake up from the most wonderful dream she'd ever had.

It was the last day of the honeymoon when Kate realized something wasn't right. Kate wanted to try snorkeling, but Antonio ranted and raved like a lunatic. He accused her of wanting to flirt with the instructor. Antonio had shown displeasure before over things he didn't agree with, but this was much different. She'd caught him on the phone with his mother later, telling the story as if she'd done something horribly wrong. It puzzled her.

The plane flight home had been no different. When Kate had tried to go to the bathroom, Antonio had suspiciously looked at her, accusing her of wanting to walk past the handsome man sitting nearby. Shortly after that, no matter where they went together, Antonio began to watch Kate closely, remarking that she dressed improperly for other men to admire her.

Little by little, Kate began to lose touch with friends and everyone she loved. Antonio couldn't bear the thought of Kate visiting her parents, though they only lived twenty minutes away. He told her she might run into an old boyfriend while she was there. He nitpicked on the dinners she cooked; he made sure she wore clothing he bought her. He belittled her in front of his friends when they visited. Chunks of Kate's fragile self-esteem began to fall apart once again.

Kate hadn't wanted to tell her parents a thing. She'd gotten herself into this mess. What was she thinking? Antonio had charmed her with his elegant ways and impeccable manners. Who knew it was all a cover up for a very controlling monster? The worst part, she still wanted to believe in him. He bought her expensive gifts and treated her like a princess some of the time. Then the other side would emerge, leaving Kate wondering what she'd done wrong.

Mrs. Stinelli, Antonio's mother wasn't much better. She was the one person Kate thought she could confide in. Kate thought she could trust the woman with something her son had said, yet she'd betrayed Kate by telling Antonio the whole story. He'd screamed at her that night, jabbing his finger into her shoulder again and again, hurting her.

By the time their first anniversary rolled around, Ellen showed up one evening at dinnertime unannounced while Antonio's mother visited.

"Hey, Blanche," Ellen said. "Nice fur. It's a little hot outside though, don't you think?" She patted the sleeve of the expensive looking cream colored coat on the woman.

Blanche Stinelli pulled her arm away distastefully. "Please do not do that again. Skin has certain oils in it which are not good for my fur."

Ellen rolled her eyes. "Sorry. Hey, Katie, let me help you in the kitchen, okay?" Kate gave her mother a pleading look. *Please don't say anything.*

"So, Mom, what brings you out here tonight?" Kate asked, turning to the sink and pushing her sleeves up to begin washing dishes.

"Okay, you can stop the pretense," Ellen whispered quietly. "You ask what brings me out here? You're my daughter for goodness sakes. Do you realize the last time I saw you?" Ellen grasped her daughter's arm and whirled her around. "Something's going on, Kate. I'm not deaf, dumb and blind, you know."

Katie broke down then. A years' worth of tears came flooding out. "Mom, I'm so sorry," she began. "I, I just don't know what to say." She quickly tried composing herself, wiping at her tears, all the while watching for her husband to walk into the room.

"You're sorry? You're sorry?" Ellen repeated. "What on earth did you do? I can't take it, Kate. This isn't you. I see a young woman before me who's a shell of my beautiful daughter. Have you looked in the mirror? You're so skinny. And what's with the dark circles under your eyes?" Ellen gestured with her hand to her daughter's face.

Just then Antonio walked in. He walked over to Kate scooping her into his arms. "It's nice of you to stop by Mrs. Martino," he said, giving his wife a passionate kiss on the cheek. His eyes narrowed into slits.

"Kate, call me please," Ellen said, and walked past them both. "Hey Blanche," she said as she strolled past the woman sitting on the sofa in the small living room. "By the way, my hands aren't oily." And she ran her fingers through the fur coat in all directions.

It didn't take much longer for Kate to realize it wasn't going to work. One of her friends called to tell her they'd seen Antonio eating lunch with a young, pretty girl. When she confronted him about this, he'd laughed at her and said her friend was jealous and making up stories. Another time, the phone rang late one evening and a husky female voice asked to speak with her husband, but quickly hung up when Kate asked who she was. The last straw came when Kate found a woman's picture on the floor of their car under her seat while she vacuumed at the local car wash.

While he was away on business for his father's steel corporation, Kate packed her belongings and snuck back to her parents' home. And when Antonio returned, he pleaded and begged her to come back, promising his fidelity, promising her anything. Then the last thing he ever said to her, "You're never going to make it, Kate. Never. You were nothing until you met me. A stupid little girl from a stupid small town. You aren't going to get anything from me. I wish you nothing but unhappiness." And with that he'd hung up.

It had taken four years after that for Kate to even try to believe in herself again. She felt stupid and ugly, a nothing. Even after the hard work she'd done in business school and extra classes she'd taken in English and creative writing. No, nobody would want her, not in the job world or the dating world. She was used up, beaten down.

When she was twenty-six, a skinny man with a cute, crooked smile caught her eye one day while she worked at a local optician's office as receptionist. He was a patient, Steve Anderson, and was adorable, clumsy, shy and witty. He didn't try to woo her with promises, he just asked her to lunch. He was the type of man who studied her when she spoke, a good listener. Kate found herself being drawn to this simple man, questioning herself and her motives, but liking the way she felt when he was around.

When a year had gone by, and their friendship had gone no further, Kate questioned Steve.

"Don't you like me?"

"What do you mean, of course I like you."

"Then why haven't you ever done this?" And she kissed him long and hard. Steve melted into her, breathless from her assault.

"Wow, Kate," he said. "I was afraid if I did that, you'd slap me." He kissed her back this time.

~*~

I sat there in my mother's kitchen, the cup of decaf

coffee now untouched before me. Mom's eyes were red from tears reliving this painful story from my past. Dad walked into the room.

"I thought you two were baking for the craft show?" He looked over at Mom. "What is it, honey?" he asked her tenderly.

"Kate and I just visited some old ghosts. I don't think they'll be back to haunt her anytime soon though. I think our daughter has really come a long way, Ray. I think she's going to do some very great things now." Mom turned to me. "You're the potter's clay, Kate. God's going to have His way with you. Just open yourself to His love and the call He has on your life."

I stood then, and walked over to my mom, hugging her as tightly as I could. In my head were visions of dementia, old age, hot flashes, even death. But also there were visions of love, laughter and life. Dad came over to us both and we all embraced.

Chapter 6

~~~~~~

Ever After

Summer, 2003

My stomach clenched with fear and I found it difficult to breathe while the soap dripped down my body and the water trickled down the drain. I raised my right hand once again to my left breast, gingerly touching the hard, round lump I'd just discovered while showering. Thoughts pummeled my brain. *God, not now. Why?* Terrifying images filled my head: surgery, mastectomy, chemo, radiation. *Cancer, oh God, please no.*

The hot water washed over me, tears mingling while I continued to hyperventilate. Panic, raw and unyielding, took hold of me. Shutting the water off, I picked up the fluffy towel I'd laid neatly across the top of the commode, hugging it to myself, fear nibbling away all rational thought. When I stepped out of the tub and viewed myself in the bathroom mirror, I turned to the left and to the right touching my right breast, fingers probing, searching. Nothing.

I didn't need this now, didn't want this now. What woman does? There was so much going on with all the excitement of joining Bunker Publishing and my *Pietro's Song* article was doing very well. They even wanted more writings from me, and I'd never felt so happy. Little by little, my insecurity slipped away and the woman God created me to be, emerged.

Mark called to me from downstairs. "Mom, hurry up. You take so long getting ready."

The pit of my stomach curdled. We were about to go on a small family trip. Steve's parents lived out of state, and we would be driving the nine hours to visit with them in North Carolina. Our son was bringing his best friend Greg Chambers, and he was more excited about this trip than any others we'd been on.

What should I do? Call the doctor, or wait until we returned? Did I tell Steve? Mom? Keep this to myself? Uncertainty, something which had become such a central part of my character, nestled into my brain.

"I have to dry my hair," I called out. "Give me about twenty minutes and I'll be down." My fingers wanted to touch the offensive spot again, but I willed myself to stop. A sick feeling overcame me and I sunk to the floor, hugging my knees to myself and rocked like a small child trying to comfort itself.

~*~

"You're unusually quiet, Kate," Steve said as we crossed the state line into West Virginia. Mark and his friend Greg giggled and ribbed one another from the back of Steve's SUV.

"Yeah, Mom, aren't we going to play some of those stupid games you like while we're driving?"

If only you boys knew what's going on with me. "Nah," I said instead. "Just a little tired guys. You can make up something if you like." I lay back against the seat closing my eyes, closing myself off from the two men in my life.

Steve's CD played oldies, his favorite era.

I fought the urge to open up to Steve, but I didn't want to ruin this trip for him. It had been a while since we'd seen his parents. No, I'd handle this on my own, and as soon as we returned, I'd phone my doctor immediately.

191

~*~

Could it be possible a week-long visit felt like only a day or so to me? My mind had been so preoccupied with the lump I'd found, I couldn't concentrate on much else. Though it had been nice spending time with Steve's eccentric mother and father, they must have noticed I wasn't myself.

On Monday morning while I washed the mountain of clothes from our trip, I finally dialed Healthcare for Women. Denise, a lovely receptionist I'd known for many years answered immediately.

"Hi Denise, it's Kate Anderson." I felt breakfast wanting to creep up.

"Hi, Kate. What can I do for you?" Her pleasant voice usually put me at ease but not on this day.

"I need to make an appointment with Dr. Taylor. I felt a lump in my left breast." It was out. The dreaded words I never thought I could say.

"Oh, okay, Kate. Can you come in this Friday around ten?"

Friday? Could it wait much longer? "Okay, that'll be fine. See you then," I said and hung up quickly. I'd waited this long. Now to tell my husband. Since it was mid-summer,

Steve was off from his teaching job. I gathered courage and mounted the stairs from the basement.

"Steve," I called. "You upstairs?" The house felt too quiet.

"Yeah, honey, what's up?" Steve appeared in the hallway of the second floor, his dark hair in waves from his shower, a towel around him. My heart beat rapidly for a moment. This handsome man, this good man. *God, please give me strength.*

"Kate, what is it?" His smile from a moment ago was gone, replaced by a look of concern. Never good at hiding my emotions, my face always betrayed me.

"I need to talk to you," I said and burst out crying.

Steve flew down the stairs as quickly as he could, enfolding me in his arms, the clean smell of Coast soap fresh on his skin. "What's wrong, Kate?"

My sobs became louder. I was glad Mark wasn't home. I was glad he'd be spending a few days with his friend Greg.

"Oh Steve, I didn't want to ruin our trip, and I didn't tell you, oh honey, oh Steve." I rambled and tried catching my breath in between fresh sobs.

"Honey, please tell me." Steve walked me over to our

couch and we sat together while I continued crying into the sleeve of my crisp cotton blouse.

"I found a lump in my breast when I was showering the first morning of our trip. Oh God Steve. I'm so scared."

The look on his face melted my heart, a look of such compassion and tenderness, it stole my breath away. Steve gathered me into his arms and let me cry some more. When I didn't think another tear could possibly flow, I quieted myself, resting in his embrace.

"Kate, why didn't you tell me sooner? Did you make an appointment with your physician?"

I nodded. "Yes, this Friday."

"Okay, I'll go with you. Let's not panic. Let's wait and see what they say. It may not be as bad as you think." Steve blew out a huge sigh. "Have you told your mother yet?"

My mother.

"No," I said. "I don't want to scare her." I sat back against the couch, the whir of the washing machine's spin cycle loud in the stillness from below us. "Maybe I'll wait until after."

"Nonsense," Steve said. "Let's tell her together. She's

your mom for goodness sakes. She deserves to know, Kate."

It was with an extremely heavy heart, Steve and I made the drive to my parents' house later that day. Mom had a pot of coffee on when we walked through the door, and the aroma of cinnamon lay in the air.

"Thought you two forgot about us," Mom cranked as we entered the kitchen and each of us pecked her on the cheek. Dad walked in behind us, a plastic model of the ship *Titanic* in his hands.

"Look what I made for Mark," Dad said. "This was from a kit. It's pretty realistic. Check out the smoke stacks."

Mom waved her hand at him. "More rubbish. I told you Mark doesn't want your junk, Ray."

Dad appeared to be getting really good at ignoring Mom's remarks. He stood there holding the foot long replica as if bestowing a beloved prize upon me.

"He'll love it, Dad," I said, giving Mom a dirty look and taking it gently in my hands.

"Steve, you want a piece of coffee cake?" Mom asked. When my husband nodded, Mom sliced into the freshly baked crumb topping, laying a slice for each of us onto her blue willow plates.

Steve looked over at me, and giving me a nod, urged me to talk with my parents. I laid the ship down on top of Mom's table and cleared my throat.

"I have something to tell you both."

Mom spun around quickly from the counter. "Please don't tell me you're pregnant," she chuckled.

"No, that's not it." Then I told them what I'd found. My parents listened, never interrupting, concern etched onto their dear faces. I'd been wrong when I thought Mom would crumble.

"Well, then we pray about this," she said. "We give it to God, knowing He's the great physician. There's nothing too big for him, Kate."

Dad sat quietly, polishing off the rest of the cake before him at a loss for words.

"When I was sixteen," Mom said, "I found a lump. I never told you, Kate, but it turned out to be nothing. Heck, back then, our parents were so darn timid about our body parts, it embarrassed my mother more than anything."

I laughed a good hearty laugh for the first time in days.

"But if it is something," I said, looking at Mom for

strength. "What if it *is* cancer, and I have to go through radiation, chemo, and God forbid, surgery." I looked down. "What if it's so bad and I, I die?"

There, it was out. All the horrible possibilities my mind had gone over in the last week. Yes, even death was lurking in the dark recesses of my brain.

Steve lay his fork down upon his plate, his face betraying him. Usually a rock of strength, he appeared lost in deep emotions.

"Kate," Mom said, "Not even for a moment do I think we'll lose you to this. You're stronger than you know. You have the support of me and your father." She picked her coffee cup up and took a long sip. "You've got a good man here, too." Mom reached across the table, laying her hand across Steve's arm.

Sitting back against the chair, crossing her arms, that faraway look on her face, Mom said important, yet frightening words. Looking directly at Steve, she spoke.

"Did I ever tell you about the time I died?" Steve almost knocked his coffee cup onto the floor. All eyes in the room were on her. I think I stopped breathing. I knew this story well, though I'd never told Steve about it. The day I'd saved my mother's life.

"Yes, I did," Mom continued. "I had a cardiac arrest when I was younger. You know, death isn't the end. I can tell you firsthand. It's the gateway to life. We think we have to fear sickness and tragedy, but this isn't the end. No sir. It's only the beginning. . ."

~*~

Ellen Martino awoke on the clear, crisp snowy morning to a feeling of pressure upon her chest, the tightness sucking the breath from her body. She quickly dismissed the feeling, knowing she'd eaten way too much the night before. She shuffled to the kitchen, an immense feeling of exhaustion overtaking her. Ellen plopped her diet capsule into the glass of water, watching the clear liquid turn orange, then drank deeply from the glass before her. She'd gained a few pounds recently and wanted to shed them as quickly as possible. Her physician had given her a new pill proven to work. He'd forgotten to tell her, however, that as the diuretic removed the excess water from her body, so did the potassium rapidly deplete.

Her husband Ray trudged into the room, huge galoshes on his feet. "Ellen, I'm gonna go clear a path outside. It snowed about four inches through the night."

Ray gathered the snow shovel from behind the basement door, his huge parka already buttoned up tightly. "You okay, honey?" he asked. "You look a little tired."

"My stomach's bothering me a bit," Ellen said, putting a hand over her mid-section. "I should never have eaten that huge meal last night. I won't be doing that again anytime soon. I only have another ten pounds to go." She sat heavily into a kitchen chair, her head in her hands.

"You look beautiful to me," Ray said, pulling his black work gloves over his hands. "I think this diet is nonsense." He kissed her forehead and left the room, shovel in hand.

Their daughter, ten-year-old Kate, sat eating a bowl of cereal, watching Bugs Bunny on T.V. It was a Sunday morning, a perfect winter day, and church was still hours away. Ray blew a kiss to his little girl before heading outside.

"Kate," Ellen called. "You okay with cereal? You want me to make something else?"

"No, Mom, I'm fine."

"I'm going to go take a shower then," Ellen said, getting up from the table. It was an effort to make her way into the bathroom. The heavy, tired feeling hadn't diminished. Ellen turned the faucet on, letting the water flow into the stall, undressing slowly, a wave of immense dizziness overtaking her. Just as Ellen was about to get into the shower, spots of light danced into her vision, then blackness fell upon her.

~*~

Kate curled upon her father's favorite recliner, the bowl of frosted flakes soggy now on her lap, her dog, Buffy lying next to her on the floor. The Road Runner cartoon was on now, and she giggled by herself in the stillness of the living room. The sound of Dad shoveling outside comforted Kate, and she wished for a moment, they didn't have to go to church today. Just for once she'd like to sit on a Sunday morning, basking in front of the television like some of her friends did, then bundle up to play outside for hours.

A loud bang from somewhere inside the house startled Kate, and she almost dropped the bowl of remaining cereal. That was strange, she thought. Buffy awoke from a deep sleep, ran from the room and began growling and barking.

"Buffy, stop," Kate called out. The dog continued. Kate put the cereal bowl onto the end table next to her and followed the growls of her dog.

It was then Kate heard a most frightening sound. A raspy, gurgling emitted from down the hallway, a sound almost like Dad when he snored so loudly at night. What in the world?

Buffy continued barking, and stood outside the bathroom door. Kate heard the sound of water running, and as she approached the bathroom, the awful gurgle grew louder.

"Mom?" Kate called. "Mom, you okay?" Nothing. It was then Kate found her feet and quickly raced outside to her father. Throwing open the front door, she screamed. "Daddy, oh Daddy, come inside. Something's wrong with Mom I think."

Ray threw the shovel down and entered the house in a matter of seconds. Pulling Buffy away from the bathroom, Ray shoved open the door and saw his wife laying half in and half out of the tub.

"Kate, call your grandma. Have her phone an ambulance. Hurry!"

Kate Martino, only ten years old, picked up the telephone and dialed *Nonna*. Broken English and all, her grandmother understood the urgency and within five minutes, an ambulance arrived at their home.

Kate watched the scene unfold, horrified, as two young men rolled a stretcher quickly past her. They wheeled her mother out before her, conscious, but groggy.

"Kate," Ellen said weakly. "You'll be okay. Mama's coming back, honey." The paramedics whisked Ellen rapidly out the door and loaded her into the back of the waiting vehicle.

It had been a long time since she'd thought of this, but Kate felt her thumb wanting to creep toward her mouth. "Daddy, what's happening?" she asked through tears which had begun to flow.

"Come on, honey," Ray said, slipping her into her winter coat. "I have to bring you to *Nonna's* house. I'll have to be with your mama for a bit now."

"Why can't I come with you?" Kate asked her father. "I'm scared."

"It'll be alright, honey. She's in good hands now."

~*~

"We're losing her! Nurse, hurry!" Ellen heard these words in a semi-conscious state. The exhaustion and heavy feeling from the morning had vanished, replaced now by a sense of floating away.

Ellen observed her body lying upon a hospital bed, while dozens of nurses ran around her. She saw from above as if she floated before this scene, watching a movie, not really participating. She felt nothing, no weakness, no pain, a sort-of disinterested curiosity at what she viewed beneath her. After a moment or so, Ellen felt herself pulled rapidly away into darkness, a winding tunnel of some sort. The faster she went, the closer a point of brilliant light started to grow. As she neared the radiance, a feeling washed over her. Later, when she returned, she'd be unable to put into intelligible words the description of such a feeling. For no words could describe the utter peace, warmth, joyful feeling that cocooned her. Ellen felt a sense of complete love and acceptance, as if she was the only person that mattered.

She sensed a presence before her, and as It was about to speak, Ellen felt herself being drawn backward as if tumbling down the shaft of the tunnel as rapidly as she'd first travelled. A loud "pop" resonated in her ears and she heard the doctor that stood before her say, "She's back."

Later that night, when Ray sat with his wife in her hospital room, the first words Ellen would say to him were: "I'm not afraid to die, Ray."

Little by little it would come out. The story of what Ellen had experienced. A doctor stopped by to speak with her and Ray explaining what had happened earlier in the day.

"You had a cardiac arrest," the doctor, still in surgical scrubs said to Ellen, removing his glasses and pressing his knuckles to his eyes. Exhaustion surrounded him, and he sat down hard in a chair near the foot of her hospital bed.

"You're lucky to be here." Looking directly at Ray, he continued. "We lost your girl for a few minutes, Mr. Martino. It appears from what you told me, she had an arrest at your house earlier today. The one she had several hours ago here in the hospital was much worse. We almost didn't get her back." The doctor rose wearily and walked over to Ray, shaking his hand.

He went to Ellen and laid his hand on her arm. "You'll be fine now. Your potassium level was nearly depleted. No more diet pills, you hear me? Whoever put you on them was careless. A diuretic depletes you of water, and if you're not putting a potassium supplement into your body, it can be devastating."

Ellen, who'd only been lying there quietly, now spoke.

"Doctor, do you believe in life after death?" She watched his face closely.

"I've seen some astounding things in my career," the doctor answered. And I'm a man of medicine and science. But yes, I think I believe there's something beyond." He turned to go.

"I was on the other side." The doctor turned to look back at Ellen.

"I felt a love like nothing I could describe. Like nothing in this world."

"You're tired, honey," Ray said to his wife. "Doc, I think I'm going to head home to my little girl. She'll rest easy now, right?"

"What, you don't believe me, Raymond?" Ellen said a bit more forcefully. "I tell you, I was there. I was there, and it was indescribable."

"The nurses will take good care of her," the doctor said, ignoring Ellen's remarks. "Glad you're doing better," he said and left the room.

"Honey," Ray began. Ellen silenced him with a hand in the air.

"Please, Ray, if you don't want to hear about it, then just say so. But never ever tell me I wasn't there. I *saw.*"

~*~

After a two-day hospital stay, Ellen was released. She'd never been happier to see her young daughter. After all, had it not been for Kate, Ellen might not have still been there, but more importantly, Ellen wanted to share her perception of the afterlife with her.

Kate viewed her mother's story curiously, as one would listen to a fairy tale. Soon other family members, aunts, uncles and cousins would hear of Ellen's strange tale. Some would believe her, and others would not.

It was about that time, a book came out by a Dr. Raymond Moody called "Life After Death." In it were case studies of people just like Ellen who'd had similar stories of an afterlife upon "dying" and being brought back to this world. Some stories were even grander than Ellen's, for some people saw deceased loved ones and even spoke with the Being who welcomed them.

In a time when it wasn't fashionable to speak of such things, Ellen's near-death experience, as these came to be known, changed her forever in a positive way. Ellen always knew when someone needed to hear her story. Someone she'd meet who was afraid of death and dying. Someone who'd lost a dear loved one. It was her personal testimony and way of helping them realize there was so much more. . .

~*~

"So you see, Steve," Ellen finished her cup of coffee, still looking at my husband. "I don't fear death, not for myself or for any of my loved ones." Mom turned to me then. "But as for you, missy, come on, let's go into my room and pray together."

Mom led me in a heartfelt prayer of healing and restoration. She prayed not only for my health, but for me to continue to follow Jesus and trust in His word. We left that night, and I felt lighter, though uncertainty still lay before me.

Steve, who'd always been attentive, treated me with even more compassion and kindness in the next few days. While we lay in bed each evening, my husband told me how much he loved and appreciated me. He shared stories I'd never known about when he first met me, and how he never thought someone like me could care for someone like him. It made me laugh to hear this. I'd always been the insecure one, but to hear my beloved husband open up to me in this way, warmed my heart and gave me a different perspective of the man I'd always thought so calm and collected. He spoke of his concerns, but with a way of looking at this whole situation from the point of view of a man who could fix anything. He wouldn't let this beat me. He wouldn't let this beat us. If he could ward away all bad, scary events from my world by willing them away, then by God, he would do so.

Friday morning arrived too quickly for me. It took everything in me to get dressed for my appointment. With a heavy heart, I trudged downstairs to make breakfast.

"Why can't I come with you and Dad?" Mark asked, while he poured Frosted Flakes into a plastic cereal bowl. "I won't get bored, I promise." He made an innocent, pleading face, and I couldn't help but laugh. "Grandpa's going to force me to glue some kind of kit together."

"Mark, that's enough." Steve's voice was unusually gruff to our son. He sat with a newspaper propped open in front of him, a huge stack of pancakes before him. "You'd hurt Grandpa's feelings if you say something like that in front of him. He works hard to make models for you." Steven put the paper down and began cutting into the food before him, the scratch of the knife on his plate grating on my nerves.

"Mark, we shouldn't be too long," I said. "Just gonna have a few tests done, then we'll pick you up. Maybe we can go eat at Los Campeseno tonight, your favorite place." *Yes*, I thought, *that is if I still have an appetite later.*

I left the kitchen, walking out onto the back porch of our home. Birds sang sweetly on this most horrible of mornings. I plopped onto our porch swing, throwing my head back, kicking my legs out before me, trying to think as rationally as I could. *It may be nothing, it could be something.*

A few minutes later, Steve poked his head out the door. "You all ready, Kate? You need anything else inside here before I lock up?"

I shook my head. My purse sat next to me already. Sighing, I left the comfort of my swing and headed toward my husband's vehicle. Next time I see my house would it be with an even heavier heart?

We dropped Mark off at my parents' house though it was out of our way to do so. Mom waved to me from the front door, using both hands to pull up the corners of her mouth indicating a Cheshire Cat grin to me.

While Steve and I drove the thirty minutes to my appointment, he turned off the radio in the car and reached over for my hand.

"No matter what, Kate, we're in this together. I love you more now than I ever did. Whether the news is good or bad, we fight and we win, okay?"

I nodded silently while a few tears slipped from the corners of my eyes. I thought about Mom's story, about the time she'd died. I knew death wasn't the end, and maybe I was making more out of this than I should. But it took something like this to make a woman think of her own mortality.

We arrived at Healthcare for Women around nine-forty- five. The receptionist Denise greeted me with one of her biggest smiles. When she reached for my insurance card, she patted the top of my hand with her own. "Kate, don't let your anxiety get the best of you. Women walk through our doors every day and things like this turn out to be nothing many times."

I sat in a cushioned chair, tall green plants and cheerful color prints surrounding me in this waiting room with its homey facade. Steve picked up a *Time* magazine and began thumbing through it.

Precisely five minutes after ten, a small, young nurse opened the door from inside the office and called out my name.

Steve put the magazine down and looked at her. "May I please come back with my wife?"

"We have a few things to do first," she said. "We can come get you in a few minutes."

I rose, breathed in deeply and began walking to the opened door. I turned back to my husband. "Steve, I'll be okay. You wait out here please."

The nurse took me to a waiting area deeper in the building and motioned for me to step into a dressing room. "Take everything off from the waist up," she said. "Put on the cotton gown from inside the cubicle with the opening in the front. You may place your things in one of the lockers off to the side. Your room will be over there," and she pointed down the hallway.

I changed quickly, gathered my discarded clothing and purse under my arm and shoved them into the tiny space of the locker. I headed toward the room she'd shown me, catching a glimpse of a woman with a huge, pregnant belly leaving another of the exam rooms. Her husband walked beside her, smiles lighting their faces as they talked about the photographic image in their hands of their unborn child from a sonogram.

The lighting was low and pleasant in the room I

entered, soft music played in the background. The nurse walked into the room behind me. She motioned for me to sit in a chair where she proceeded to take my blood pressure reading and a quick listen to my chest with a stethoscope.

"Dr. Taylor will be in shortly," she said, closing the door, closing me off from the rest of the building, leaving me to my own little world.

In the quietness of the room, I prayed one last time. *"God, thank you for being with me today. Thank you for answered prayers and good health. I'm in your hands."* A feeling of peace overtook me. I knew, no matter what, my heavenly Father was right there with me.

Dr. Taylor, a thin, pretty woman in her early fifties, I guessed, walked through the door and shook my hand.

"Hello Kate. Today we're going to run a few tests. After establishing the area your lump is in, I'll do the ultrasound first, then we'll ship you across the hall for a mammogram. Once I check the films, if I feel anything further should be done today, we may have to prepare you for what's called fine needle aspiration. Now, don't let this scare you. These are procedures which are done every day. This may turn out to be nothing serious."

I lay back on the table while the doctor ran a rather cold, hard object over my breast again and again. It wasn't painful, but I didn't care much for the sensation. She made cheerful small talk as she worked, and I found myself liking this woman very much indeed.

When she was through, the nurse from earlier took me across the hallway and proceeded to perform a regular mammogram.

After this, I was ushered into a small waiting area where a few other women milled about, some, patients like me, and others, nurses. An elderly woman who sat next to me began chatting about her life, telling me she was here for a follow up from a recent mastectomy. I listened intently to this dear lady who spoke intelligently and upbeat. She'd survived cancer, she told me, and fought long and hard. She was in remission and wasn't going to let this stop her. She had eight grandchildren who needed her and she wasn't planning on going anywhere.

Despite the seriousness of the moment, I felt completely at ease and relaxed when Dr. Taylor poked her head into the room. "Kate, would you follow me, please?" Six little words that could change my life. She led me into the room the ultrasound had been performed in.

"Well, so far, I think we have some pretty good news."

A huge sigh escaped me. I don't think I could have been any happier. "What does that mean, doctor?"

"The on-site radiologist read your films and your ultrasound already. When our patients live farther away as you do, we try to determine as much as we can on the same day." She motioned for me to sit in the chair and pulled the little wheeled stool in front of me.

"From all accounts, it appears to be a fatty cyst. We'll know more once we perform the needle biopsy. Unfortunately, you won't know the rest of the results today, but from what I can see, and what the radiologist read, I think you'll be okay."

"Would you be able to send my husband back?" I asked.

"Let's get this procedure done first, Kate. You won't be very long."

Several nurses scampered into the room, preparing me for the next leg of my journey. An on-site anesthetist came into the room, preparing to numb the area. Others milled about, wheeling carts to and fro, and hooking me up to an intravenous solution.

The doctor explained where the needle would enter my skin. Then a very thin, hollow tube attached to a syringe would drain fluid from the cyst in my breast. The results would be sent for further testing, and I'd be free to leave after a short recovery.

I lay upon the table as she worked, several nurses chatting amicably in the room, thinking back on the last several years. I'd grown closer to my parents in my forties. The love between my husband and I was stronger than ever. Even though life brought its ups and downs, the closeness of family mattered most. I had a healthy son, a really good kid. I had a job I enjoyed and a possible writing career ahead. Though some frightening, sad, and otherwise negative moments from my past had been revisited recently, I had so much life ahead of me, so much to look forward to.

A little later in the recovery room, Steve stood next to me, smiling that gorgeous smile of his, stroking my arm with his fingertips as we waited for news of when we could leave. He'd been thrilled with the initial good news, and though we had to wait a few days for the results of the biopsy and possibility of minor surgery to remove the offensive cyst, he looked more relaxed then he'd been in days.

~*~

When the phone rang later in the week, and I answered out of breath after running from the basement, the words from Dr. Taylor were balm to my ears. There was no threat of cancer. The cyst was due to the onset of menopause, a fibrocystic change. There hadn't been any blood present in the fluid she'd drained, so there was a good chance the cyst would resolve on its own. When I hung up, I dropped to my knees thanking God, knowing He wanted me here for a much longer time.

~*~

On my forty- fourth birthday, Mom threw me a huge surprise party. My brother, Matt, his lovely wife Tina, a few cousins, my son, husband and closest friends celebrated my life. My very good life. And as Mom and I cleaned up a little later, she hugged me tightly.

"Kate, I'm very proud of you. You've always been my shining star. I love you so much."

As I sat back in my mother's kitchen with a cup of coffee and a piece of my birthday cake, I looked at Mom and thought: *When I grow up I want to be just like you.*

Recipes from Ellen's Italian Kitchen

The following recipes were dictated to me by my mother when I was first married in my early twenties. As you may see, they aren't from any book, but given directly from a loving mother to her daughter as she begins her baking journey. If you have any questions, please feel free to email me at scoutfinch15003@yahoo.com.

Wine Cookies

1 cup sugar

1 cup dry red wine

1 cup oil

2 tablespoons Crisco or shortening

1 teaspoon lemon extract

4 ½ cups flour

Make a well in flour either in large mixing bowl or directly on a dough board. Add all other ingredients directly into this. Mix well. Shape like small doughnuts. Dip tops in bowl of white sugar. Bake on floured cookie sheets. 350 degrees for 30-35 minutes.

Lemon Knots

Makes a flaky, pie-crust type sugary cookie.

6 eggs, beaten

1 cup oil

1 ¼ cup sugar

1 cup milk

2 teaspoons lemon extract

6 teaspoons baking powder

Pinch of salt

6 cups flour

Beat first five ingredients together. Mix flour, salt and baking powder separately. Mix all together and turn out on board. If too soft, add a little more flour.

Cut off long pieces and roll like log. Form as in a knot, like small pretzel.

Bake 10-12 minutes at 350 degrees.

When cooled, mix powdered sugar and milk with a ¼ teaspoon of lemon extract to a runny, but semi-thick consistency. Dip tops of cookies into mixture and place aside to harden.

Italian Easter Bread

An old Italian favorite. Great with coffee!

2 sticks butter

2 ½ cups milk

3 packages dry yeast (not quick raise)

6 eggs

2 cups sugar

Grated orange peel

1 ½ teaspoon anise oil (extract)

In a small bowl, place 1 ½ cups warm water. Sprinkle all yeast into it and add 1 teaspoon sugar to it. Set aside.

In small saucepan heat the milk and butter. Simmer, don't bring to boil.

In large mixing bowl place 2 cups sugar. Pour the hot milk and butter over sugar and stir until sugar dissolves. When milk cools a little, add 3 cups flour and about ¼ cup oil at this point. (Makes sponge) Add grated orange peel and anise.

Beat eggs in separate bowl, add to flour mixture and add the yeast mixture into flour at this point.

Begin adding the rest of the flour and kneading it until it doesn't stick to hands. Can coat hands with a little oil as kneading.

Raise in mixing bowl covered with clean dishtowels and soft blanket until finger presses down and it doesn't indent. This will probably be a couple hours.

Place in greased loaf pans or make rolls in 13 x 9 pan. Raise one more time, covered. Set oven to 350 degrees.

Beat another egg in bowl with small amount of milk. Coat tops of bread right before baking with egg and milk wash. Bake 20-25 minutes, but keep checking oven when you see the tops browning. Sometimes I cover with aluminum foil to slow down the browning.

The aroma in your kitchen from this bread will make your family come running. This bread is excellent sliced and toasted. Don't forget to slather butter when it's warm.

About the Author

Karen Malena is a daughter, wife and mother living in Western, Pennsylvania. Her compassion toward others is evident in her writings and blogs. Her interests include reading, weekend trips with her husband, music and nature. Karen is active in her town encouraging others to write through local library programs and author events. She's a member of Pittsburgh East Scribes and Ligonier Valley Writers.

Other books by Karen Malena

Shadow of my Father's Secret

2013 Concerning Life Publishing